Clinical Negligence and Complaints

A clinician's guide

Clinical Negligence and Complaints

A clinician's guide

Michael Green BSc, LLB, PhD Solicitor

Smith Llewellyn Partnership, Swansea

Kathryn McConnochie BSc, MB ChB, MRCP, LLB Barrister

Pendragon Chambers, Swansea

The ROYAL
SOCIETY *of*
MEDICINE
PRESS *Limited*

The purpose of this book is to provide a summary of the law and practice of clinical negligence litigation and complaints. It can deal with matters only in general terms. As each case is different practitioners faced with a complaint or litigation should seek the help of their defence organisation or NHS Trust managers for advice about specific cases.

British Library Cataloguing in Publication Data
A catalogue record for this book is available from the British Library

ISBN: 1-85315-504-7

Typeset by Phoenix Photosetting, Chatham, Kent

Printed in Great Britain by Bell and Bain Ltd, Glasgow.

▶ Contents

▶ ABBREVIATIONS

AC	Appeal Cases
All ER	All England Law Reports
BMLR	Butterworths Medical Law Reports
CA	Court of Appeal
Lloyd's Rep Med	Lloyd's Law Reports: Medical
Med LR	Medical Law Reports
QBD	Queen's Bench Division
WLR	Weekly Law reports

▶ Preface

Have you ever received a letter like this ...

Dear Dr Dangerous,
I am writing to complain in the strongest possible terms about your disgraceful and negligent treatment of my self/mother/brother ...

... if you have, or worry that you will, then this book is for you.

Our aim is to shed light on what happens when a complaint is made. We take you through the NHS complaints procedure and into the solicitor's office. Along the way, we hope that you will gain an understanding of how clinical negligence lawyers think and how you can avoid finding out first-hand.

Between us, we have considerable experience of both working in the NHS and acting in clinical negligence claims. Perhaps by reading this book you will put us out of work. It's a risk we are prepared to take. To the best of our knowledge and belief, the law is stated correctly as at 1st March 2002.

Michael Green, Solicitor.
Dr Kathryn McConnochie, Barrister

June 2002

1

Background

For knowledge itself is power
Francis Bacon 1561–1626

Introduction

It is difficult if not impossible to work in the health care sector without being aware of the vast increase in complaints from patients and their relatives. Most of these complaints are resolved at local level but some turn into legal suits. The prospect of a brush with the legal profession is one that many health care workers would rather avoid. Surprisingly, therefore, until very recently, clinical litigation has not had a high profile either with successive governments or at local level. There is no shortage of serious academic input into medical law and ethics but ask, for example, a junior hospital doctor what actually happens when a patient makes a complaint or takes a complaint to a solicitor to discover there is plenty of concern, a willingness to learn, but almost no knowledge. Most health care organisations arrange occasional visits from interested solicitors and extracurricular lectures on legal matters to groups of health care workers are always well attended. However, in the past year or so, the Government has set up a number of organisations and commissioned several reports concerned with mistakes, complaints and clinical negligence. The effects of these are starting to filter down to the front-line and may lead to a sea change in culture. In the meantime, we have filled this book with information that we hope you will find useful in understanding the present system and how to survive it.

Size of the problem

Fenn et al[1] estimated that hospital NHS claims cost £52.3 million in the year 1990–1991. In a further study published in 2000, Fenn et al[2] analysed data collected from NHS hospitals in the Oxfordshire Health Authority. They found that the rate of closed claims increased during the 1990s by around 7% per annum. Their best estimate is that clinical negligence, including defence expenditure, cost the English NHS between £48 million and £130 million (95% confidence interval) in 1998. By extrapolation, outstanding liability for currently open claims is around £1.8 billion.

Any serious clinical negligence lawyer could have told the Government years ago that compensation payments are increasing exponentially. Thankfully, this sort of anecdotal evidence is at last being matched by proper well-researched figures albeit sometimes extrapolated from research work from Australia and the USA.

The facts are alarming so it is surprising that very little accurate information is available from UK medical practice. In the past year or so, the Government has set out to try to address this gap in our knowledge.

New initiatives

New initiatives are aimed at several areas of concern:

1. mistakes – how to report
              how to learn from them
              how to avoid
2. NHS complaints procedure
3. disciplinary measures for doctors
4. clinical litigation
5. compensation schemes.

Mistakes

In its report, *An Organisation with a Memory*,[3] the Department of Health estimated that each year:

*   400 people die or are seriously injured in adverse events involving medical devices
*   nearly 10,000 people are reported to have experienced serious adverse reactions to drugs
*   around 1150 people who have been in recent contact with mental health services commit suicide
*   nearly 28,000 written complaints are made about aspects of clinical treatment in hospitals
*   the NHS pays out around £400 million a year in settlement of clinical negligence claims, and has a potential liability of around £2.4 billion for existing and expected claims
*   hospital-acquired infections – around 15% of which may be avoidable – are estimated to cost the NHS nearly £1 billion.

Equally sobering, the same report estimates that in NHS hospitals alone adverse events in which harm is caused to patients:

*   occur in around 10% of admissions – or at a rate of 850,000 a year
*   cost the service an estimated £2 billion a year in additional hospital stays alone, without taking any account of human or wider economic costs.

The stimulus for this report came from several sources most notably the public outcry at the thirteenth death from maladministration of drugs by spinal injection, which was particularly shocking given the publicity surrounding previous similar errors. Other doctors who had made this error before had faced manslaughter charges though these were subsequently dropped.

It is accepted in the report that '... high risk medicine is bound to be eventful and that serious errors and complications will never be eradicated'.[3]

An Organisation with a Memory was followed by *Building a Safer NHS for Patients* (http://www.doh.gov.uk/buildsafenhs), which recommended the setting up of the National Patient Safety Agency. This organisation came into being in April 2001 and runs a mandatory reporting system for mistakes, errors and near-misses. Its website at http://www.npsa.org.uk is a likely source of useful information but has yet to reach its full potential.

Another new body, the Commission for Health Improvement (CHI) has been set up under the Health Act 1999. Part of its remit is to investigate failures of systems within the NHS but not individual complaints, which should be taken to the NHS complaints procedure. For example, CHI published a comprehensive report (http://www.chi.nhs.uk) in August 2001 of their investigation into failures of systems and procedures following the conviction of Peter Green, a GP from Loughborough, on nine counts of indecent assault. CHI found, 'An NHS complaints system failing to detect issues of professional misconduct or criminal activity.'

To complement the CHI and the General Medical Council (GMC), of which more later, and following recommendations from the Chief Medical Officer, the Government has also established the National Clinical Assessment Authority (NCAA). Details of the role of the NCAA can be found on its website at http://www.ncaa.nhs.uk. In essence, its job is to deal with concerns about doctors in difficulty, undertake assessments of such doctors and help resolve the problems identified. Unlike the GMC, the NCAA is not a regulatory body. In December 2001, the CHI, GMC and NCAA published a Memorandum of Understanding setting out the position of each body and how they will work together. As the NCAA is not yet in full flow, we have yet to see whether these bodies will work together in practice. The NCAA, for the moment, only covers NHS doctors and doctors working for the prison service in England. Dentists may be included in the future.

These initiatives are part of the slow recognition within the health care sector that there must be a cultural change towards openness and admission of errors. Of course, it has been said, with some justification, that it is difficult to admit errors when these admissions can lead straight to the law courts.[4] It is in recognition of this inevitability, that the Government has at last started to intervene.

In a recent lecture to University College London the Lord Chief Justice, Lord Woolf[5] examined the courts' changing view of the medical profession. This has mirrored the change in public opinion from a traditional acceptance that 'doctor knows best' to a demand that medical practice become more open and accountable. Lord Woolf said, '... it is unwise to place any profession or other body providing services to the public on a pedestal where their actions cannot be subject to close scrutiny.'

One of the difficulties is that few people outside of medicine can appreciate how sensitive doctors are to criticism. Generally speaking, this has nothing to do with arrogance or status, it's much more fundamental. It may rest in the fact that doctors are trained to believe in themselves and the choices they make in a way unknown in other walks of life. This training allows a doctor to make and live with daily decisions, which affect life and limb. The down side is that criticism becomes personal, not something to be dealt with at arms length. Perhaps it would be better if doctors were more immune to criticism but at what cost.

How do clinicians get the balance right? Should every trivial mistake be admitted? In the rush towards openness, it is easy to forget that 'healing the sick' is a complex interaction between the 'healer' and the 'sick'. It is quite different from the kind of relationship you may have with the car mechanic at your local garage whose ability to fix your car doesn't depend on any form of emotional interaction. You still like to have confidence that the job has been done correctly. Would you have that confidence if the mechanic told you of every dropped nut or wrong spanner chosen? If the job was satisfactorily completed with no detriment to your car or your pocket what does it matter?

In medicine, the situation is much more complex. A patient's ability to tolerate an unpleasant procedure may depend in part on their confidence in the operator. Compliance with drug treatment is often better where there is a good relationship between doctor and patient. To a great extent, patients want and need to trust their doctor. In the rush towards this new culture, care should be taken not to destroy or render ineffectual the capacity of doctors to treat illness.

The problem can be summarised thus:

- balancing the need to retain trust and confidence
- advising whether a mistake is negligent
- differentiating adverse incidents from unsatisfactory outcomes in a way which retains public confidence.

A mistake or negligence or an undesirable outcome?

Clinical negligence lawyers spend a lot of time explaining the difference between mistakes, negligence and undesirable outcomes to potential litigants.

The legal concept of negligence is described in detail in Chapter 2. Suffice to say for the moment that not every mistake is negligent. To some extent, the unsatisfactory outcome is more difficult to deal with. Patients' expectations have never been so high. A patient who remains in pain after a routine hip replacement operation is often certain that something has gone 'wrong'. That may be right or it may be that everything went to plan but something unforeseen has led to the unsatisfactory outcome. Even when an independent assessor finds no negligence, patients by and large remain convinced there was some error.

The following practical examples demonstrate the difficulties:

- Mistake or negligence?
  Mistake: Perforation of the uterus during routine curettage.
  Negligence: Perforations of the uterus during routine curettage with additional damage to some other organ such as the bowel.

- Negligence or poor outcome?

  Negligence: Failure to warn that a new treatment for raised blood pressure can cause permanent loss of taste in 15% of patients and loss of taste occurs.

  Poor outcome: New treatment for raised blood pressure fails to work.

NHS complaints procedure

It is widely accepted that the present system is failing both complainants and the complained against. In Chapter 3 we look at how it works and how to deal with the present scheme.

Disciplinary measures for doctors

Regulatory bodies, in particular the GMC, have had a torrid time. The GMC is in the midst of a major restructure. Whether this will be sufficient to fend off increasing calls to end self-regulation for doctors remains to be seen.

Clinical litigation

The wind of change is blowing through the world of complaints and clinical negligence, and not before time. Public confidence in the NHS is at an all time low. The reasons that patients turn to law are multifactorial not least that legal action, however blunt a tool, provides a way to complain and to seek redress.

This has been of major concern to the Government and culminated in the National Audit Office (NAO) report of May 2001, *Handling Clinical Negligence Claims in England*[6] and the setting up of a committee led by Professor Liam Donaldson to examine the options to the present system. The Department of Health asked for views and comments from interested parties by 10 October 2001. At the time of writing (March 2002), the White Paper is still awaited (for further information see (http://www.doh.gov.uk/clinicalnegligencereform/index.htm).

In summary, the NAO found there were around 10 000 new claims in 1999–2000. The rate of new claims per thousand finished consultant episodes rose sevenfold between 1995/6 and 1999/2000. At March 2000, provisions to meet likely settlements for up to 23 000 outstanding claims were £2.6 billion. It was estimated that a further £1.3 billion was needed to meet settlements for claims that could arise from incidents that have occurred but have not yet been reported. This figure of £3.9 billion was increased to £4.4 billion in the most recent (NHS) England Summarised Accounts 2000–2001.[7]

The NAO report made several recommendations. Of particular interest, the Department of Health should give clear guidance to NHS Trusts on what information they may give to patients who have suffered adverse incidents, including those who may have suffered negligent harm. The Department of Health had said that they do not see it as the business of the NHS to advise patients that there might on the face of it be grounds to believe an adverse medical event may be due to negligence, or suggest patients seek legal advice, or admit liability (see page 4 'Conclusions (b) 12 in ref 6). In reality, it is not unknown for staff to tell a patient that something has gone wrong. Clear guidance on this point would at least provide a uniformity currently lacking and could contribute to a more open culture within the NHS.

It remains to be seen how the NHS will implement any direction to advise patients of adverse incidents. The difficulties will be deciding what level of adverse incident should be notified, though the indication from the National Patient Safety Agency is that all failures, errors and near-misses across the health service will be logged.

Compensation schemes

Unfortunately, the remedies available to patients often fail to meet their expectations. Whilst many patients will admit that they want money, even more want an admission of fault and an investigation into what went wrong. As things stand, with very few exceptions, if a patient wants any money, they have to follow the litigation path.

Many difficulties stem from the fact that there is no communication between the clinical complaints procedure and clinical negligence litigation. They are currently regarded as being mutually exclusive and yet each has something different to offer.

What the complaints procedure can offer:

Easy to initiate
Investigation whilst events are still fresh in everyone's mind
Opportunity to improve practice and procedures
No financial consequences for the complainant
Less likely than litigation to disrupt the doctor–patient relationship
Generates paperwork which can be used should litigation follow
A range of non-financial remedies such as an apology.

What clinical negligence litigation can offer:

Financial recompense.

A further interesting recommendation in the NAO report is that the Department of Health, the Lord Chancellor's department and the Legal Services Commission should further investigate alternative ways of satisfactorily resolving small and medium-sized claims, for example through the offering of the wider range of non-financial remedies that patients say they want, setting up regional panels and offering mediation where appropriate. As things stand, the Department of Health have a policy of not allowing patients to pursue both a legal claim for an award of money and go through the hospital complaints procedure at the same time. Given the choice, and fearful that delay may prejudice their chance of securing financial compensation, many patients forego the hospital complaints route and so lose out on the opportunity to get any explanation or apology. Nobody knows the extent to which this occurs. It is possible that a change in approach whereby most potential claimants also seek a hospital enquiry could swamp the system.

Whistle-blowing

The plight of the whistle-blower within the NHS received widespread publicity following the Bristol Enquiry. It is hoped the Public Interest Disclosure Act 1998 will encourage and protect health care staff who want to report their concerns. Whistle-blowers now have statutory protection if they disclose information reasonably and responsibly in the public interest.

Despite this, there is still a widespread reluctance to blow the whistle. It is not part of NHS culture. For one thing, too much depends on patronage of one sort or another and no one likes a possible troublemaker. Doctors in training who are often well placed to identify problem consultants are also the most vulnerable.

Recently, the CHI published its own whistle-blowing policy to 'provide a framework to promote responsible whistle-blowing'. This is a welcome move and may serve as a template for other bodies who wish to follow suit.

The future

Given that the Government is committed to publishing a White Paper on clinical negligence this year it is perhaps of limited value for us to either speculate or anticipate. However, many of the proposed remedies are already being discussed publicly and it so it may be useful to briefly look at the pros and cons.

No-fault compensation

As things stand, if you are injured as a result of a medical procedure, you have to show that health care providers were somehow at fault before you can claim compensation. If, for example, a medical procedure was competently performed but due to some unforeseeable circumstance you end up with a significant disability, you will not be eligible for compensation. In many countries, this is considered unacceptable. In New Zealand, for example, there is no need to show 'fault' before accessing compensation. On paper, 'no fault' compensation appears so attractive that it is difficult to see why it has not been adopted everywhere. In practice, as has been found in New Zealand, there are many difficulties. 'No fault' compensation schemes are very expensive, cases are not necessarily resolved any more quickly and the level of compensation awarded may be insufficient to meet the needs of the injured party.

Settlement procedures

Another proposed remedy is to deal separately with claims of low and medium value. Regional panels could award compensation to a given ceiling and could recommend non-financial remedies. Alternatively, NHS Trusts could be empowered to do the same thing.

An obvious objection to these proposals is that patients will lose their access to independent medical and legal advice. If that access is preserved, then the creation of panels may do no more than create a two-tier and more expensive system. That being said, it seems likely that the Government will look closely at the current well-established scheme to administer compensation to victims of criminal injury. Tariffs for various injuries, a cap on the total amount of compensation that can be awarded and dealing with lower value claims on paper will surely figure in any new proposals. The fact that these possibilities may not address patients' needs for apologies, explanations and reassurances begs for further debate.

It is not the remit of this book to explore the culture of complaint further but the interested reader is directed to the references at the end of the book. We both believe that change will come but hope, perhaps optimistically, that it will be driven by the needs of patients and health care workers rather than political expediency. We shall see.

References

1 Fenn P, Hermans D, Dingwall R. Estimating the cost of compensating victims of medical negligence. *Br Med J* 1994; 309: 389–391.
2 Fenn P, Diacon S, Gray A, Hodges R, Rickman N. Current cost of medical negligence in NHS hospitals: analysis of claims database. *Br Med J* 2000; 320: 1567–1571.
3 Department of Health. An organisation with a memory. Report of an expert group on learning from adverse events in the NHS. London: The Stationery Office, 2000.
4 Turnberg L. To err is human: learning from mistakes. *Clin Med JRCPL* 2001; 1: 264.
5 Lord Woolf (2001) 9 Medical Law Review.
6 National Audit Office. Handling clinical negligence claims in England. Report by the Comptroller and Auditor General HC 403 Session 2000–2001: 3 May 2001. London: The Stationery Office, London.
7 Civil Court Service [2001] Laws *et al.* Jordan Publishing. (Reproduced with permission).

2
Basic law

The first thing we do, lets kill all the Lawyers.
Henry IV Part 2
Shakespeare 1564–1616

Introduction

This chapter will examine some basic elements of law as they are applied to matters medical. Much of the material which follows, particularly areas such as negligence or causation, applies to civil claims generally and is simply imported into the medical context. Negligence, for instance, is part of the general law of tort. As the criminal law confers upon the State the ability to apply sanctions to individuals in respect of their wrong doing, so the law of tort provides a mechanism of redress between individuals. Examples include the torts of libel, trespass and negligence. In each case, before a successful claim can be brought, a causal link must be demonstrated between the act of the wrong doer and the harm caused to the individual bringing the claim. As with most aspects of civil claims, the burden of proving liability in the case falls to the claimant who must prove his case to the court upon balance of probabilities.

Some claims are brought under statutory provisions such as the Fatal Accidents Act 1976. Such statutory claims are usually brought in addition to claims brought in common law. An important aspect of bringing a claim is the fact that certain time limits apply. The manner in which these limits operate is to set a time by which a claim must be commenced at court. If the claimant fails to bring his claim within the prescribed time then, usually, the defendant is protected from suit. Limitation is an important but complex area of law which we will look at in greater detail.

Of considerable significance to both sides of a claim is the level of damages which the claimant would recover if successful. We will, therefore, consider the level of damages awarded to successful claimants and how those damages are calculated. Finally, we will consider an aspect of the law with little application outside of the clinical setting. This is consent to treatment.

Background

The law of England and Wales is derived from three main sources. These are: statute (Acts of Parliament), case law precedent and, more recently, Europe. An Act of Parliament becomes law by being passed through both houses of Parliament, the House of Commons and the House of Lords and receiving Royal Assent. During this passage through Parliament each proposed piece of legislation is scrutinised and amended to produce (in theory at least) workable, sensible law. Many Acts of Parliament, known as primary legislation, contain provisions allowing Ministers to make more detailed regulations dealing with the subject matter of the Act. These regulations are known as subordinate or secondary legislation and are usually passed as Statutory Instruments. The details of the parliamentary process are beyond the scope of this book.

England and Wales operate a Common Law system of law. The term is derived from the days when the assizes were held throughout the country and the judges would tour around each 'Circuit' sitting at the various centres of population. As different judges might, on different occasions, apply the law as they understood it slightly differently, it was agreed between the judges that they would attempt to apply the same law in all the courts and rely on each other's decisions to set precedent. It was this 'common' approach that gave rise to the 'Common Law'. We have, therefore, a system of case precedents where decisions of courts on the same level are persuasive but the decisions of the higher courts are binding on the lower courts. Thus the decisions of the House of Lords on a given point will bind all courts below. Such decisions are, therefore, referred to during trials by advocates in the hope of swaying the judge in their favour based on appropriate precedent.

The other obvious advantage of a precedent system is that it provides a degree of certainty to the parties. Such an approach allows lawyers to advise their clients as to the likely outcome of any given case. Always remember, however, that approximately 50% of the parties who go into court end up losing!

The legal system in England and Wales in broadly divided into two sectors. The first deals with criminal matters and the second with civil matters.

The lowest tier of criminal courts is the Magistrates Court. It deals with less serious criminal matters, youth crime and has a jurisdiction for certain child care cases. The cases are heard by lay magistrates (addressed as Sir, Madam or Your Worships). All serious criminal matters are tried at the Crown Court. These cases are heard with a Judge (addressed as Your Honour or My Lord) and a jury. There is a middle band of offences which are known as 'triable either way' where the defendant (not the prosecution) can elect a jury trial (at the moment at least).

The civil courts deal with claims between individuals, companies, government bodies etc. The lowest tier of the civil courts is the County Court. It now has wide ranging jurisdiction. Civil claims in the county court are divided into three tracks. The small claims track deals with cases where the monetary value is less than £5000. These claims will be heard by District Judges (addressed as Sir or Madam). Generally, legal costs are not available in the Small Claims court. Fast-track cases are those where the monetary value is over £5000 but less than £15000 and the trial can be heard in less than 1 day. The trials are heard by District Judges and/or Circuit Judges (addressed as Your Honour). Generally, legal costs are available but are limited in the fast-track cases. The highest County Court track is the multi-track. Multi-track cases are unlimited in financial value and in trial length. Multi-track cases are usually heard by a Circuit Judge (addressed as Your Honour). Cases which are known to be of some complexity and/or are of high financial value are usually issued in the High Court.

There is little practical difference between cases run in the High Court and cases run in the County Court. High Court cases are heard by High Court Judges (addressed as My Lord). In both the multi-track cases and High Court cases, legal costs are available and are within the discretion of the court.

Negligence

In everyday conversation, the word negligence is often used synonymously with carelessness. However, in a legal context, negligence has a specific meaning. For the courts to make a finding of negligence against a doctor, or for that matter anyone else, three elements must be present within the facts of the case. These are:

- a duty of care
- a breach of that duty
- foreseeability of harm.

Duty of care

> The cardinal principle of liability is that the party complained of should owe to the party complaining a duty to take care, and that the party complaining should be able to prove that he has suffered damage in consequence of a breach of that duty.
>
> Per Lord MacMillan in *Donoghue -v- Stevenson*[1]

Mrs Donoghue and a friend visited a café in Paisley where her friend ordered for her a 'ginger beer float'. The bottle of ginger beer was opened and poured over the ice cream which Mrs Donoghue consumed. The remains of the ginger beer were then poured from the bottle and it became apparent that there was a foreign body in the bottle. It was alleged that the central, but unnamed, character in *Donoghue -v- Stevenson* (the foreign body), was a former snail. Mrs Donoghue was made ill by the partly decomposed snail, the thought of it, or both. As Mrs Donoghue was not the purchaser of the ginger beer, she had no contractual relationship with the seller. She decided to pursue a claim against the producer of the ginger beer. Part of the argument before the court was whether or not a duty of care could be owed by the producers of the ginger beer to a consumer where they would have absolutely no idea of the identity of that consumer at the time the ginger beer was manufactured and bottled. This led Lord Atkin to put forward his 'neighbour principle' which states that you must take reasonable care to avoid acts or omissions which you could reasonably foresee would be likely to injure your neighbour. In this context, a neighbour is anyone who is likely to be affected by your act or omission such that you should have them within your contemplation at the time of your action or inaction. Thus, a driver of a car clearly owes a duty of care to other road users.

It is easy to see that a consumer of a bottle of ginger beer, whoever they may be, should be owed a duty of care by the manufacturer. Such a wide duty is, of course, seen in pharmaceutical and other product liability cases where a duty is owed to any potential consumer. The courts have, however, been reluctant to extend a doctor's duty of care to all unidentifiable potential 'victims' of the doctor's default. In *Palmer -v- Tees Health Authority & Hartlepool & East Durham NHS Trust 1999*,[2] a claim brought by the mother of a murder victim failed. A psychiatric patient who was discharged from hospital was alleged to have told staff that he had sexual feelings for children and had the inclination to murder a child. The victim of the patient had no prior connection with him so the court struck out the claim holding that the duty of care did not extend to all unknown potential victims of the patient's actions.

It may also be the case that the doctor's duty of care extends beyond merely the patient. The case of *McLoughlin -v- O'Brian* (See appendix 2)[3] established what is known as the 'aftermath principle'. The aftermath principle envisages the case where a patient dies as a result of clinical negligence in the presence of a close relative of the patient. The shock of witnessing the manner of the death of the patient causes nervous shock to the relative for which they can recover damages. The nervous shock must, however, be more extensive than the normal grief which a relative might suffer due to the non-negligent death of a loved one. It has, however, been held by the courts that the relatives of a deceased patient cannot recover psychiatric injury from a doctor who provided information in relation to the death of a patient (*Powell -v- Boladz*[4]).

While each doctor owes a personal duty of care to their patients, in the case of treatment provided by a doctor in the course of their employment by an NHS Trust, the Trust is vicariously liable for the acts of its agents or servants and is, usually, named as the defendant.

An NHS Trust can be liable as a defendant in its own right if it fails in its duty to provide adequate staff to ensure the proper care and safety of its patients. This duty cannot be delegated to another body even if the care of the patient in question is contracted out to the private sector (*M. V. Calderdale -v- Kirklees Health Authority*[5]).

In a medical context, a duty of care is often easy to establish. The doctor–patient relationship clearly places the doctor in a position where a duty of care is owed to the patient. That duty then extends not just to diagnosis and treatment but also to advice given to the patient in a medical context. In *Gold -v- Haringey Health Authority*,[6] Mrs Gold alleged that she had received negligent advice relating to the failure rate of a sterilisation operation. It was held that the Bolam[7] test should apply both to contraceptive advice and therapeutic advice. At the material time, there was a body of responsible medical opinion which would not have warned as to the potential failure of female sterilisation. The defendants were not, therefore, liable. It must, however, be remembered that a patient–doctor relationship must exist before the duty can arise. Generally speaking, a doctor who happens to come upon the scene of a traffic accident is under no obligation to assist the injured parties. If, however, the doctor does decide to help in commencing assessments or treatment of the casualties, the doctor assumes a duty of care by which he is then bound not to make the victim's condition worse.[8]

It is, however, difficult to establish when a patient–doctor relationship arises. In *Barnett -v- Chelsea & Kensington Hospital Management Committee* (See appendix 2)[9] it was held that the hospital owed a duty of care to a person who presented himself at the casualty department even though he had not yet been in any sense admitted to the hospital. Summaries of these cases are in Appendix 2.

Breach of duty

Having established whether or not a duty of care exists, it is now necessary to establish what a doctor must do, or indeed not do, to be in breach of that duty. The test applied by the courts is commonly known as the 'Bolam' test. It can be summarised:

> *Where you get the situation which involves the use of some special skill or competence, then the test as to whether there has been negligence or not is not the test of the man on the top of a Clapham Omnibus, because he has not got the special skills. The test is the standard of the ordinary skilled man exercising and professing to have that special skill ... a man need not possess the highest expert skill; it is well established law that it is sufficient if he exercises the ordinary skill of an ordinary competent man exercising that particular art.*
> Per McNair J. In *Bolam -v- Friern Hospital Management Committee*
> (See appendix 2)[10]

It can be seen from the above quotation that there is no counsel of perfection. The standard expected of doctors, and other professionals, is that of the ordinary competent practitioner.

The standard having been set, the next question to pose is, how is the level of skill of the ordinary competent doctor to be judged? In seeking to answer this question it is useful to consider the following:

> *In the realm of diagnosis and treatment there is ample scope for genuine difference of opinion and one man clearly is not negligent merely because his conclusion differs from that of other professional men ... The true test in diagnosis or treatment on the part of a doctor is whether he has been proved to be guilty of such failure as no doctor of ordinary skill would be guilty of if acting with ordinary care ...*
> Per Lord President Clyde in *Hunter -v- Hanley*[11]

It is clear from the above quote that the courts will not decide between two schools of thought in medical practice. A doctor should not be held negligent simply by virtue of his preference of one acceptable mode of treatment over another. This does, at first sight, appear to provide medical professionals with an easy route via which they can escape liability. This is because it is generally sufficient for a defendant to demonstrate that there is a responsible body of similarly qualified practitioners who would have acted as the defendant did under the circumstances prevailing at the material time. This position remains but has been slightly modified by the case of *Bolitho -v- City and Hackney Health Authority.* (See appendix 2)[12]

In *Bolitho*, the court held that while, generally, where a defendant is supported by distinguished experts, he is not negligent, it is open for the court to analyse whether or not the position adopted by the defendants and the supporting experts is reasonable. It is open to the court to decide that the body of medical opinion upon which the defendant relies has no logical basis and cannot, therefore, absolve the defendant of responsibility. A defendant relying on outdated or unreasonable practices will be found liable.

The application of the 'Bolam' test by the courts and the way in which it relies on medical opinion often gives rise to a public perception that the medical profession closes ranks and protects its own. It is certainly true that the way in which the courts apply the test means that there is no absolute standard by which the profession is judged. However, this is arguably a good thing in that as technology and practice changes with time the standard by which medical professionals are judged changes accordingly. Each act of alleged negligence is considered in the light of reasonable practice at the time when the alleged negligent act or omission occurred. In *Roe -v- Minister of Health,* (See appendix 2)[13] the court considered a case where the claimant suffered paralysis as a result of spinal anaesthetic being contaminated by phenol. Although the incident occurred in 1947, the risk of this happening was not made public until 1951. It was not possible for the defendant to have known that this risk existed at the time he administered the anaesthetic. The claimant therefore failed. As an aside, it is almost certainly the case that the court achieved the correct result but invoked the wrong theory. It is more likely that it was the pH of the solution which caused the harm and not the phenol.

As the NHS comes under increasing financial pressure, the resources available to adequately treat patients become stretched sometimes to breaking point. Is it, therefore, open to health care providers to argue that they were not in breach of their duty to their patients as they did their best with the limited staff and other resources available? The answer from the courts is a categorical no. In *Bull -v- Devon Area Health Authority* (See appendix 2)[14] the court was asked to consider the adequacy of the defendant's system for the provision of experienced obstetric cover in the event of a normal, but multiple birth. The first of uniovular twins was delivered but experienced staff were not readily available to deliver the second twin within a reasonable time (20 minutes) of the birth of the first twin. The second twin suffered brain damage as a result. The fact that the obstetric registrar on duty at the time had to cover two hospitals, on two separate sites was no defense to the delay in help arriving.

Foreseeability of harm

For the defendant to be held negligent, the claimant must show that it was foreseeable that the act or omission complained of would cause some harm of the nature of the harm suffered by the claimant. The exact harm suffered by the claimant does not have to be foreseeable, just that the claimant would suffer harm of that particular sort. If, for instance, a patient was at risk of developing a thrombosis and the treating doctor negligently failed to prescribe appropriate anti-coagulation therapy, it would not matter whether the patient suffered a stroke, pulmonary embolus or heart attack or even all three. It is sufficient that the foreseeable consequence of a clot developing was that one or more of those events could occur.

A point worthy of note is that the extent of damage that was foreseeable is irrelevant. It does not help the defendant if damage of a foreseeable nature occurs to an extent way beyond that which could have been predicted.

Causation

To bring a successful claim, the claimant has to show not only that negligence occurred but that the negligence caused an injury to the claimant. It is at the hurdle of causation that many claimants' cases fall. The claimant may be able to show that they received substandard care but this, alone, is not enough. It is the substandard care which must directly lead to the harm for which compensation is recovered.

This position is neatly illustrated by *Barnett -v- Chelsea & Kensington Hospital Management Committee* (See appendix 2).[15] Mr Barnett, who was a night watchman, complained of abdominal pain and vomiting after drinking tea. He was taken to the defendant's hospital where the casualty officer negligently failed to treat him. He subsequently died of arsenic poisoning. His widow brought a claim against the hospital, which failed. The judge concluded that whatever the casualty officer had done, it was unlikely that an effective antidote would have been administered to Mr Barnett in any event. In short, he would have died anyway.

Several cases have come before the courts where doctors have negligently failed to diagnose a fetal abnormality. Successful claims have been brought by claimants who have argued that they were denied the opportunity to terminate the pregnancy in question. However, where the defendant has been able to show that this particular claimant would not have agreed to a termination in any event, the claim has failed. Similarly, if the negligently performed test was carried out after the time when a termination could have been legally performed, the negligence of the defendants had no causative effect.

The claimant does not, however, have to show that the negligence complained of was the sole cause of his injury. He can often succeed where there are other potential causes at play provided he can show that the breach of duty made a 'material contribution' to the injury suffered by the claimant (*Bonnington Castings Ltd -v- Wardlaw*[16]). Where, however, several competing causes for the claimant's injuries exist, if the claimant cannot show that it was the 'negligent cause' rather than any other which resulted in or made a material contribution to his injuries, then his claim fails. Thus in *Wilsher -v- Essex Area Health Authority* (See appendix 2)[17] a baby suffered retinopathy and claimed that it was due to a negligently excessive supply of oxygen. Upon the evidence before the court, it was apparent that there were a number of competing causes, any one of which may have been responsible for the unfortunate claimant's condition. As the claimant was unable to show which, if any, of the potential causes was responsible for the retinopathy, the claim failed.

Occasionally, the position is slightly more complex in that it is alleged that a failure to act results in injury. The court must then enquire as to what the doctor in question would have done had they acted and then whether what the individual doctor would have done can be supported by a responsible body of medical opinion (*Bolitho -v- City*

& *Hackney Health Authority*[18]). The courts have, traditionally, seen causation on an all or nothing basis. There is, generally, no compensation for the loss of a chance. An example of this is to be found in the case of *Hotson -v- East Berks Area Health Authority* (See Appendix).[19] In *Hotson*, a child fell and sustained a slipped epiphysis. The diagnosis was negligently missed. The evidence before the court, however, was that, in any event, there was a 75% prospect of long-term harm resulting from the fall. The claimant could not, therefore, show that upon balance of probabilities, i.e. greater than *50%*, the negligence made any difference. Even if the condition had been diagnosed promptly, there was only a 25% chance of avoiding the longer term complications in any event. The claim, therefore, failed.

Very rarely, a claimant can seek to rely on the doctrine of *res ipsa loquitur* (the thing speaks for itself). In essence, the claimant is arguing that where there is no possible non-negligent cause of the injuries, the fact that the injuries have occurred or an injury has occurred indicates that negligence must have occurred. To defeat such plea, the defendant simply has to show that there is a possible non-negligent mechanism which would result in the claimant's injury. The defendant does not, however, have to prove that this non-negligent mechanism actually occurred.

An example of a successful plea of *res ipsa loquitur* is to be seen in *Woodhouse -v- Yorkshire Regional Health Authority.*[20] Mrs Woodhouse was a pianist who underwent two operations, the first in January and the second in February 1976, under the care of the defendants. In the first operation, her left ulnar nerve was damaged and in the second her right ulnar nerve suffered similarly. The neural damage resulted in severe contracture deformities of her fingers. The court concluded that ulnar nerve damage was a well known complication of operations carried out under general anaesthetic. Protecting a patient from such injuries, if carried out correctly, is almost always successful. The judge concluded that the standard precautions could not have been taken and so found for Mrs Woodhouse.

Subject to the principle that an injury must be foreseeable, the extent of the harm caused is irrelevant. This is generally known as 'thin skull rule'.

One who is guilty of negligence to another must put up with the idiosyncrasies of his victim that increase the likelihood or extent of damage to him; it is no answer to a claim for a fractured skull that its owner had an unusually fragile one.

Per MacKinnon L. J. in *Owens -v- Liverpool Corporation*[21]

Occasionally, the chain of causation can be broken by an event unconnected with the original negligence. Such an event can either occur naturally, be the act of the claimant or the act of a third party. Once the chain of causation is broken, the negligent defendant either becomes totally relieved of liability or has his liability significantly reduced to only that portion of the claimant's injuries or damage for which he was directly responsible. One example would be where a negligently performed spinal operation rendered the claimant incapable of work. Under those circumstances, the defendant would be liable for the claimant's injury and consequential loss of earnings. If, however, before the case was settled the claimant suffered a heart attack which would, in any event, have rendered him incapable of work, the original defendant would be liable for damages in respect of his paralysis and loss of earnings up to the date of the heart attack but not thereafter.

A second example might be where a hospital negligently fails to diagnose cancer in a patient who, before he suffers any serious harm from the disease is killed in a road traffic accident. Under those circumstances, the liability of the hospital in damages would be minimal and the claim for the patient's death and consequent financial loss would rest with the negligent motorist. Where such a third party act is involved, lawyers often refer it to as a *novus actus interveniens*. Whether or not the chain of causation is broken in any particular case is a question to be decided by the court on a case by case basis relying partly on case precedent and partly on public policy. For instance, in *Emeh -v- Kensington & Chelsea & Westminster Area Health Authority*, (See appendix 2)[22] Mrs Emeh, who already had three healthy children, became pregnant following a failed sterilisation operation. She refused to have a termination of the pregnancy but brought proceedings against the defendants in respect of the birth of her fourth child. The Court of Appeal reversed the trial judge's decision and held that her refusal to undergo a termination of the pregnancy was not so unreasonable so as to break the chain of causation. The defendants' argument that the claimant failed to minimise her damage also had little impact on the court.

There could, in rare circumstances, be a case where the defendants claim that the negligence of the claimant has contributed to their own downfall. Such an argument frequently succeeds in reducing the defendants' liability in more general personal injury claims but has not been used in the clinical negligence context in the UK. This is probably because of the difference in knowledge and skill which exists between the average layman, who is generally the claimant, and the medical profession. It would, however, probably assist the defendant to advance such an argument where, for instance, the claimant has flatly refused to follow medical advice and made his condition significantly worse. A similar situation arose in the Canadian courts and served to reduce the damages received by a claimant. In the case of *Crossman -v- Stewart*,[23] the claimant, Mrs Crossman received a prescribed drug which, due to lack of medical supervision, damaged her sight. The damage was exacerbated by the fact that she obtained an alternative supply of the same drug which she took without the knowledge of her treating doctors. Mrs Crossman was held to be two-thirds to blame and her damages were reduced accordingly. In many ways, this overlaps with the duty to mitigate ones' loss which will be discussed further under the heading of damages.

Burden and level of proof

The general rule is that he who asserts must prove. It is, therefore, for the claimant to prove every limb of his case. He must do so to the civil level of proof which is 'upon a balance of probabilities'. This simply means is it more likely than not that things occurred the way the claimant says so. A 51% likelihood is enough. This should be contrasted with the standard of proof required in a criminal case which is 'beyond reasonable doubt'. The legal rationale behind this should be clear. In a civil claim, the court is asked to decide between the parties who are, in the eyes of the court, equal. The court must simply decide which one is right. The higher standard in criminal cases results from the recognition of an imbalance due to the fact that it is usually the State bringing a case against an individual where the consequences for the individual, if convicted, are often dire. Hence the greater degree of certainty being required.

Limitation

Limitation is the legal concept which regulates the time the claimant has to commence proceedings in court after the incident complained of. It has long been recognised by the courts that the longer the period of time allowed to elapse between the incident complained of and trial, the more difficult it is for the parties to adduce cogent evidence. The reasons for this are obvious, memories fade and documents, even (if not especially) medical records, get lost.

The Limitation of Actions generally is governed by the Limitation Act 1980. The whole subject of limitation is extremely complex and so only a brief overview can be considered here.

The Limitation Act provides that the primary limitation period in respect of personal injuries is 3 years from the date on which the cause of action accrued or the date of knowledge (if later) of the injured person. Section 14 of the 1980 Act provides that the date of knowledge, which starts the primary limitation period running, is the date upon which a person first knew that he had a significant injury which was attributable, in whole or in part, to the act or omission alleged to constitute the negligence. The claimant does not have to know that he actually has a claim at law.

Time does not run against a person who is under a disability. For our purposes, persons under a disability will generally fall into two categories. The first are minors. When a cause of action accrues whilst the potential claimant is a minor, limitation begins to run when the individual reaches the age of majority, currently 18 years old. The claimant has, therefore, effectively until their 21st birthday to commence proceedings.

The second major group of people under a disability are often referred to as 'patients'. These are persons who are incapable of managing their affairs because they are suffering from 'mental illness, arrested or incomplete development of the mind, psychopathic disorder, and any other disorder or disability of the mind' (s.1(2) of the Mental Health Act 1983). If the cause of action accrues during a period of time when the potential claimant is under a disability, time does not start running until the disability comes to an end. Where a claim arises from a death, the 3-year period commences from the date of death or the date of knowledge of the personal representatives or dependents.

Occasionally, a claimant can issue proceedings outside of the limitation period and ask the court to exercise its discretion to allow the proceedings to continue even though they were issued out of time. The discretion is provided by Section 33 of the Limitation Act. Section 33 has often come to the rescue of a solicitor who would, but for the exercise of the court's discretion, themselves be negligent for failing to issue the proceedings in time. In fact, the courts have recently moved towards the view that a proposed claimant should not be penalised for the ineptitude of his solicitors. Section 33 provides that in considering whether or not to exercise its discretion, the court should have regard to all the circumstances of the case and in particular to:

- The length of and reasons for the delay on the part of the claimant.
- The effect which the delay will have on the quality of the evidence.
- The conduct of the defendant which may have contributed to the delays.
- The duration of any disability which the claimant was under after the cause of action arose.
- How promptly the claimant acted once he realised that he could have a claim.
- The steps which the claimant took to obtain medical and legal advice.

The limitation period in respect of civil claims arising from injuries caused by an assault or battery is 6 years. This period cannot be extended by the discretion of the court. This is because assault and battery are deliberate acts. A battery is an unauthorized physical contact, while an assault is where the victim is caused to fear that a battery is about to occur, whether contact takes place or not. Thus to punch a victim from behind so he doesn't see the punch coming is a battery, but not an assault. However, to throw a punch which does not connect, but which the victim sees, is an assault. A punch which the victim sees and which also connects is an assault and battery. By the same reasoning, unauthorized surgery, while the patient is anaesthetized, constitutes a battery. Assault and battery are both torts and crimes.

Similarly, a claim based on negligent medical advice, which does not, of itself, cause personal injuries would also have a 6-year limitation period. An example would be where someone was negligently advised to give up work but then it subsequently turned out that they were not suffering from the condition upon which the negligent advice was wrongly based.

Damages

Unfortunately, the court cannot turn back the clock or physically make good any damage sustained by a claimant. In this context, all a court is able to do is award financial compensation for the injuries and losses a successful claimant has sustained as a consequence of the negligence of the defendant. The aim of the court is, as far as is practicably possible, to place the claimant in the position that he would have been in had the negligence not occurred. In appropriate circumstances, it is open to the court to award punitive damages. These are generally known as aggravated or exemplary damages. The award of such damages is usually confined to cases where the behaviour and motives of a public body are brought into question in the case. An example would be wrongful arrest and malicious prosecution by the police. It is very rare that a court awards punitive damages in a clinical negligence context.

Damages for personal injury are usually dealt with under two headings: general damages and special damages.

General damages

General damages are awarded in respect of pain, suffering and loss of amenity. Traditionally, the method by which the court assesses general damages is to rely on precedents. Faced with a particular injury, for instance the loss of sight of one eye, a judge would look to the level of damages previously awarded for a similar injury and then, if necessary, bring the award up to date by the use of inflation tables based on the retail price index. More recently, the Judicial Studies Board have issued guidelines that seek to categorise injuries of each type, into mild, moderate and severe and set a bracket within which such awards should be made. These guidelines are published in a booklet which is widely available.[24]

It has long been recognised that if the awards in respect of injuries are compared between jurisdictions on a like for like basis, the awards in the UK tend to be quite low. This recently led to a recommendation by the Law Commission that general damages should be increased. In February and March 2000, the Court of Appeal considered together a number of separate appeals selected to provide the court with injuries covering a wide spectrum of severity. This led to recommendations by the court that the level of damages in respect of injuries should be increased where the injury would have attracted £10,000 or more before the case was heard *(Heil -v- Rankin* [25]*)*.

The tradition of using first precedents and, more recently, the guidelines means that there is a greater degree of certainty in the estimation of general damages by the lawyers of both the claimant and the defendant. Arguments do, however, still occur. It is, obviously, in the interests of the claimant to argue that his particular injury is towards the higher end of the bracket and for the defendants to suggest that it is to the lower end of the bracket.

Special damages

Special damages relate to losses which can, in theory at least, be calculated precisely. This would include, for instance, loss of earnings, loss of pension rights and continuing nursing care. The court tries, as far as is possible, to calculate the actual loss to the claimant under each head of damage. Where past losses are concerned, say by way of loss of earnings, this is relatively straight forward. If, at the time of trial, the claimant has been out of work for 4 years and, pre injury, took home £1000 a month, his past loss of earnings would be £48,000. Where, however, the claim relates to future earnings, two major difficulties immediately spring to mind. The first is that life, itself, is inherently uncertain. People can lose their jobs at any time, and for all sorts of reasons. For the defendant to pay the claimant their loss of earnings in full up to retirement age would place the claimant in a far stronger position than he would have been in had the accident not occurred. This is especially so in the case of a young claimant. The second point is that by having the projected loss of earnings paid as a lump sum at the time the case concludes, the claimant benefits from the accelerated payment in that they can then invest earnings which they would not have received perhaps for some 20 years. Again, this would unjustly benefit the claimant. The mechanism by which these problems are overcome is the use of tables that take account of actuarial information and the rate of return which can be achieved on investments. A rate of return of 4.5% used to be considered the appropriate value. But following the decision of the House of Lords in *Wells -v- Wells*[26] a figure of 3% return was adopted. This has recently (27 June 2001) been reduced to 2.5% by the Lord Chancellor using his powers under s.1 of the Damages Act 1996. Future changes to the rate may, of course, occur. With the lower predicted rate of return on the investment, it is clear that a greater capital sum is required to make good the claimant's loss. This is reflected in the table producing a higher multiplier.

To perform a calculation of special damage which is ongoing, an annual value for each head of ongoing damage is taken. In our example of loss of earnings, this would be £12,000 per year. This is known as the multiplicand. The multiplier is then selected from the tables depending on the age of the claimant at the time of trial and the rate of return that is being applied. The multiplier is then used to produce the final figure for each head of damage.

More recently, particularly in the case of very large claims where there is an ongoing and high cost of care, structured settlements have been arranged. In essence, these involve taking a significant portion of the capital and using it to purchase an annuity that generates sufficient income for the life of the claimant to cover the recurrent annual costs. This provides a safety net for the claimant in that the money should never 'run out'. This, unfortunately, does not always work in practice. Other potential solutions, such as periodical payments are currently being considered.

Occasionally, a court can be asked to make an award of damages on a provisional basis. This will occur where the court is persuaded that the claimant's condition may well deteriorate over a given period of time. It would, therefore, be manifestly unfair to the claimant to settle the claim on his present condition when he may require far more help in the future. At the time of trial the court will award damages on the claimant's current condition but provide in the final order that the claimant can make further applications to the court in respect of additional damages within a specified period of time.

Finally, mention should be made of interest. Interest on general damages is awarded at 2% from the date on which the proceedings were served to the date of trial. The provision of interest on special damages is slightly more complex. As far as past losses are concerned, interest is paid at half the appropriate rate over the relevant period. This is because some of the loss would have accrued immediately after the injury, whereas some would not have accrued until just before trial. Half the prevailing interest rate is therefore a reasonable compromise. The interest rate applied is the High Court special investment account rate prevailing at the relevant time, currently 7%.

In conclusion, it would be useful to mention a few matters which may be of interest to the reader. The first is the provisions of Section 2 of the Law Reform (Personal Injuries) Act 1948. This provides inter alia that in calculating medical expenses, for instance the cost of further surgery, nursing care, or physiotherapy, the claimant is entitled to ignore NHS facilities and recover, from the defendants, the private cost of treatment. Clearly, the defendants argue that for the claimants to be paid in such a way results in a 'double recovery'. There is no mechanism which exists to prevent a claimant recovering the private costs of his surgery and then going on to have the surgery performed on the NHS. The defendants clearly consider this to be an injustice. It also does not sit well with the concept of mitigation of loss. As a general rule, an injured party cannot sit back and try to recover all of their losses from the defendant. They have a duty to keep those losses to a minimum. Where, for instance, the claimant has been rendered incapable of performing their original job, they should seek to secure employment of a more suitable nature. Their loss would then be reduced from their full loss of earnings to the difference between their earnings originally and their earnings in their new employment, post accident.

Consent to treatment

The basic premise which underpins the law of consent is that of the autonomy of the individual. Each person has a choice. This choice can manifest itself as an expression of preference for one form of treatment over another, or, in the extreme, a refusal of treatment altogether. In the vast majority of patient–doctor encounters it does not feature overtly. A patient attends the surgery, outpatient clinic or ward, is advised of the most suitable treatment and, without further ceremony, follows that advice. There are, however, occasions when life is not that straightforward. One such occasion may be where an emergency arises during treatment where prompt action is required and there is no time to observe fully the legal niceties. An example of this may be a serious haemorrhage during childbirth. Here the doctor has to act promptly in the best interests of the patient.

As a general rule, the treatment of a patient requires his consent. The consent is usually required to be given by the person who is the subject of medical treatment. Rarely, however, consent may be given by a third party who has lawful authority to grant such consent, an example being a parent consenting to treatment on behalf of a child. Spouses and the parents of adult patients do not, in the vast majority of cases, have any authority to consent on behalf of their spouses or adult children. The exception being certain treatment within the context of the Mental Health Act.

The law of consent has three functions:

1. It protects the interest of the patient in providing that an adult patient of sound mind has the right to determine the nature and extent of any treatment, which they will undergo.
2. It protects the interest of the doctor. If valid consent is obtained it is a defence to allegations of battery.
3. It helps to establish, as between the doctor and his patient, the boundaries of treatment recommended by the doctor that are acceptable to the patient.

For valid consent to be obtained a number of elements are necessary. Each of these elements can be considered in turn.

The patient must be legally competent

To be competent, a patient must be aged 16 years or older (Family Law Reform Act 1969) and not suffering from any condition which affects his ability to reach a rational decision. Incapacity could be brought about by various circumstances including mental illness, conditions affecting intellectual function (e.g. hypoglycaemia) or unconsciousness. A patient is presumed to have capacity to consent unless and until that presumption is rebutted (*Re MB*).[27]

Consent must be "real"

Consent that is obtained by misrepresentation or undue influence is unlikely to be upheld by the courts. In *Freeman -v- Home Office (No 2)*,[28] Sir John Donaldson considered the position of a prisoner who claimed that his consent to medical treatment was not real consent because of what he perceived to the influence over his life, which could be exerted by the doctor in question. Similarly, consent, which was obtained by deliberate fraud, was not valid consent (e.g. *Appleton -v- Garrett*[29]).

The person consenting must be suitably informed

The question of 'informed consent' is clearly of great significance to both patients and practitioners alike. How much does a patient have to be told for it to be considered that they have been properly informed? The answer lies in the judgement of the House of Lords in the case of *Sidaway -v- Board of Governors of the Bethlem Royal Hospital and the Maudsley Hospital* (See appendix 2)[30]. The House of Lords, in a majority decision, set out the following principles for the guidance of both doctors and the courts:

> A doctor's duty of care to his patient when advising him about a particular course of treatment is the standard of the ordinary skilled man exercising and professing to have the special skill which that doctor is exercising and professing to have ('Bolam' test).
>
> It is a matter of clinical judgement to determine what degree of disclosure of risks is best suited to assist a particular patient to make a rational choice as to whether or not to undergo a particular treatment.
>
> Whether or not a failure to disclose a risk or cluster of risks in a particular case constitutes a breach of the doctor's duty is a matter to be decided principally on the basis of expert medical evidence. Having heard the evidence it is for a judge to decide whether a responsible body of medical opinion would have approved of non-disclosure in the circumstances of the case.
>
> A judge may come to the conclusion that, even in the absence of expert witnesses, disclosure of a particular risk was so obviously necessary to an informed choice on the part of the patient that no reasonably prudent medical man would fail to make it.

The advantage of applying the "Bolam" test to the question of providing patients with information upon which to base their consent is that the law is able to keep pace with changing standards in medical and surgical practice over the years. The judge will determine any disputed issue principally on the evidence of practitioners practicing in the same field as the doctor whose standard of professional care has been called into question and will be concerned only with evidence of the standard which was appropriate at the time of the incident complained of.

> *The doctor cannot set out to educate the patient to his own standard of medical knowledge of all the relevant factors involved. He may take the view, certainly with some patients, that the very fact of his volunteering, without being asked, information of some remote risk involved in the treatment proposed, even though he describes it as remote, may lead to that risk assuming an undue significance in the patient's calculations.*
>
> Per Lord Bridge in *Sidaway -v- Board of Governors of the Bethlem Royal Hospital and the Maudsley Hospital* [31]

A similar view was taken by Lord Diplock (in *Sidaway*) when he said:

> *To decide what risks the existence of which a patient should be voluntarily warned and the terms in which such a warning, if any, should be given, having regard for the effect that the warning may have, is as much an exercise of professional skill and judgement as any other part of the doctor's comprehensive duty of care to the individual patients.*

In *Pearce -v- United Bristol Healthcare NHS Trust* [32] Lord Woolf said:

> *If there is a significant risk which would affect the judgement of a reasonable patient, then in the normal course it is the responsibility of the doctor to inform the patient of that significant risk, if the information is needed so that the patient can determine for him or herself as to what course he or she should adopt.*

Unfortunately, this approach creates many unanswered questions. For instance, what level of risk is significant? Lord Woolf suggested 0.1% would not be, but 10% would. Also risk of what? A stiff leg for 3 days or permanent paraplegia?

While the aim of the clinician should always be to act in the best interest of the patient and to provide the best care possible, the legal position can never be ignored. By far the most satisfactory solution is to follow a practice which serves the patient and, at the same time, protects the practitioner. This must involve, wherever possible, an early and thorough explanation of the treatment options including the effects of non-treatment. If appropriate, some of the things which could go wrong may be discussed in advance. The information provided to the patient should be recorded along with any preferences expressed by the patient. This is particularly important where there is unlikely to be a chance for the patient to reassess the position once treatment is underway.

Adults incapable of giving consent

Clearly, the Mental Health Act 1983 provides for certain circumstances where persons may be detained against their will and, if necessary, treated for their mental disorders within the terms of the Act. The Act does not, however, set out what the law is when a patient is incapable of understanding what is being suggested to him. Prior to 1960 the Crown had the power and the duty to protect the person and property of those unable to do so for themselves. This prerogative jurisdiction was revoked by the coming into force of the Mental Health Act 1959. The statute, unfortunately, put nothing in its place.

In *Re F*[33] the House of Lords considered the power of a court to authorise a sterilisation of a mentally incompetent adult woman. F was a voluntary patient at a mental hospital. She was 36 years old with the mental capacity of a child of 4. She had become involved in a relationship with a male patient but medical staff felt that a pregnancy would be 'disastrous from a psychiatric point of view'. The House of Lords concluded that in these circumstances sterilisation was permissible and lawful since it was within the patient's 'best interests'. 'Best interests' was to be taken in a wide sense so as to include public interest but in the area of non-therapeutic sterilisation was not to include the convenience of those responsible for a patient's care.

The House further held that the test to be applied to the lawfulness of such an operation and of other treatment carried out for adult persons or who are incapable of consent is that laid down in *Bolam*, namely that a doctor will not be negligent if he acts in accordance with responsible medical practice current at that time. The House of Lords further held that the High Court had the power, in its inherent jurisdiction, to make a declaration as to the lawfulness of treatment provided to an adult who was unable to give a valid consent. It said that as a matter of practice, though not of law, the opinion of the court should be sought as to the lawfulness of a sterilisation operation on an adult woman of child bearing age who is incapable of giving or refusing her consent herself. In his speech, Lord Goff stated:

> *The overriding consideration is that they should act in the best interests of the person who suffers from the misfortune of being prevented by incapacity from deciding for himself what should be done to his own body, in his own best interests.*

He also suggested that there should be little difficulty in applying this principle in the case of routine treatment of mentally disordered patients. Where the proposed treatment was more serious, it was likely that good medical practice would involve discussions with others before the final decision was taken. This would usually include relatives and others who are concerned with care of the patient. On a practical note, if the agreement of relatives is sought and obtained then it is far less likely that any legal challenge to the validity of the decision to carry out any treatment or procedure will be forthcoming.

The doctrine of 'best interests' was examined again by the House of Lords in *Airedale NHS Trust -v- Bland* (See appendix 2)[34]. This case involved an unfortunate victim of the Hillsborough Disaster who was suffering from a persistent vegetative state as a result of injuries which he had sustained.

The House of Lords held:

1. That the object of medical treatment and care was to benefit the patient. A large body of informed and responsible medical opinion considered that the persistent vegetative state was not for the benefit of the patient. The principle of the sanctity of life, which was not absolute, was not violated by ceasing to give medical treatment to which the patient had not consented and which conferred no benefit upon him.
2. That the doctors responsible for the patient were neither under a duty, nor entitled to continue such medical care since the patient had no further interest in being kept alive.
3. Until a body of experience and practice had been built up it was desirable that applications should be made to the Family Division in any case where medical staff considered that continued treatment of the patient in a persistent vegetative state no longer conferred a benefit upon him.

Children

A young person can be treated as an adult at 16 years of age and can be presumed to have the capacity to decide to give or withhold consent. Under 16, a child may have the capacity to decide depending on whether or not they can understand what is involved. However, if a competent child refuses treatment, then either a person with parental responsibility or the court can authorise investigation or treatment which is in the child's 'best interests'. If a child under 16 is not competent to decide, then a parent can consent on their behalf. However, if the person with parental responsibility refuses treatment on a child's behalf that you consider to be in that child's best interests you can seek a ruling from the court. In emergency, if you think it is in the child's best interests, you can treat the child in so far as it is required (see *Gillick* below).

Emergency treatment

There are times when the condition of a patient requires rapid intervention, often to save his life. On such occasions, it is not uncommon for the patient to be unconscious or otherwise unable to give valid consent.

In *Gillick -v- West Norfolk & Wisbech Area Health Authority* (See appendix 2)[35] Lord Templeman said:

> *A doctor may safely carry out treatment in an emergency if the doctor believes the treatment to be vital to the survival or health of an infant. In such a case the doctor must have the courage of his convictions that the treatment is necessary and urgent in the interests of the patient and the court will, if necessary, approve after the event treatment which the court would have authorised in advance even if the treatment proves to be unsuccessful.*

In *Re F*,[33] Lord Goff took the matter a little further. He said that in emergency treatment a conservative approach should be adopted:

> Where, for example, a surgeon performs an operation without his consent on a patient rendered temporarily unconscious in an accident, he should do no more than is reasonably required, in the best interests of the patient, before he recovers consciousness. I can see no practical difficulty arising from this requirement, which derives from the fact that the patient is expected before long to regain consciousness and can then be consulted about longer term measures. The point has, however, arisen in a more acute form where a surgeon, in the course of an operation, discovers some other condition which, in his opinion, requires operative treatment for which he has not received the patient's consent. In what circumstances he should operate forthwith, and in what circumstances he should postpone the further treatment until he has received the patient's consent, is a difficult matter, which has troubled the Canadian courts but which is not necessary for your Lordships to consider in the present case.

The nature and extent of treatment administered to a patient in an emergency, and without his consent, seems to be limited to that which is necessary to save his life and, presumably, restore him to a position where he is able to provide consent for further treatment. Whether or not any particular procedure or treatment falls into this category will, inevitably, be judged by the *Bolam* standard. In other words, would a responsible body of skilled professional opinion have considered that the treatment administered was appropriate and necessary at the relevant time?

Except in the case of children or consent given by the courts, the consent of a third party has no legal effect. However, the doctor is likely to reduce the risk of any adverse legal consequences of his actions if the views of close relatives are canvassed before treatment is undertaken.

Refusal of consent by an adult

Recent cases have indicated that the courts have been ready to intervene to sanction treatment which has been refused by an adult patient. The court has considered itself able to act in this way by applying the 'best interests' principle.

In *Re T*[36] the court considered the case of a 20-year-old woman who had been brought up by her mother as a Jehovah's Witness. She had signed a consent form in which she had refused to consent to a blood transfusion following a road traffic accident. Her mother had been with her for much of the time following the accident before her condition had deteriorated. Her condition became critical and she was sedated and placed on a ventilator. The Court of Appeal held that although an adult patient was entitled to refuse consent to treatment irrespective of the wisdom of her decision, for such a refusal to be valid the treating doctors had to be satisfied that at the time of the refusal her capacity to decide had not been diminished by illness, medication, false assumptions or misinformation, that her will had not been overborne by the influence of another person and that her decision had been directed to the situation in which it had become relevant.

The court held that on the facts of the case the patient's refusal was not effective as it had been overborne by her mother's wishes and the refusal was given before her condition deteriorated to the point where it became critical. Lord Donaldson added that doctors and health authorities should not hesitate to apply to the court for assistance in cases of doubt as to the effect of a reported refusal of treatment where a failure to treat would threaten the patient's life or cause irreparable damage to their health.

An interesting example of an adult refusing treatment is to be found in *Re C* (See appendix 2)[37]. C was, at the relevant time, 68 years old. He suffered from paranoid schizophrenia and was a patient detained under the Mental Health Act. He was diagnosed as having gangrene in his right foot. He was transferred to a general hospital for surgery. He refused an amputation stating that he would rather die than have his leg removed. The Trusts made an application to the court for an order that the surgery could proceed without his consent. The court found in favour of C. It was held that notwithstanding his mental condition, he was able to understand and retain the information relating to his intended treatment. It was further stated that the Mental Health Act only permitted compulsory treatment for his mental condition and nothing else.

Research

Medical research may be divided into two broad headings:

● therapeutic – i.e. research carried out on patients.
● non-therapeutic – i.e. research carried out on healthy volunteers.

There is no reason, in theory at least, why the principles of consent that apply to ordinary therapeutic treatment should not also apply to both therapeutic and non-therapeutic research.

Consent in non-therapeutic research is probably the easiest to deal with in that it involves healthy volunteers who are, by their very nature, able to give valid consent limited only by the proviso that they receive a clear indication of the likely effects of the treatment they will undergo and the risks attendant upon that treatment.

It is, arguably, slightly more difficult in the case of therapeutic research in actual patients. Take, for instance, the question of a drug trial where the effects of a drug on a condition are being compared with the effects of a placebo. In a properly constructed trial, none of the participants will know which patients are receiving the placebo. It must, therefore, be carefully explained that participation in the trial may actually work to the detriment of an individual patient.

The position is even worse in the case of research on children and mentally incompetent adults. Only the court can consent to medical treatment on behalf of the mentally incompetent adult except where the 'best interests' of the individual are clearly satisfied by the need to treat. It certainly cannot be the case that taking part in a trial can be said to be in the best interests of that patient. This is, therefore, as much a question of ethics as it is of law.

Advance treatment directives or 'Living Wills'

The significance of advanced treatment directives or 'Living Wills' has grown over the last few years. The validity of such directives has often been questioned both by lawyers and the medical profession. In fact, the position is not as complex as it may at first, appear. The position is that a patient who can consent to or refuse treatment now is equally capable of consenting to or refusing treatment for the future. There is certainly no legal reason why that should not be the case. There are, however, a few practical difficulties which arise from advanced treatment directives. The first is, clearly, ascertaining the wishes of the patient in question. This can be relatively straightforward if the circumstances under which treatment is to be consented to or refused are foreseeable at the time of your consultation. Take, for example, the case where a patient's condition is likely to deteriorate and they state, categorically, that they do not wish to undergo resuscitation in the event of a cardiac arrest. That can, quite clearly, be noted within their medical records and the appropriate staff alerted at the time. The same 'do not resuscitate' instruction is more difficult to deal with where an emergency arises and the treating staff are not familiar with the patient in question. Under those circumstances, in the absence of knowledge of the patient's wishes, the staff would have to proceed and would be allowed to proceed with emergency treatment as with any other patient. Similarly, where there are religious or other objections to blood transfusions, and those views are known, the patient is within their rights to state that they will not consent to a transfusion under any circumstances in the future. Where such a declaration is known to the treating medical staff, then it must be respected. The medical staff cannot, however, be held liable for ignoring an instruction the existence of which they were not aware.

It is likely that an advanced treatment directive, particularly one made in writing, would be valid even if the patient, at the time of treatment, was suffering from a mental or physical condition which meant they were no longer able to appreciate the gravity of their present situation. As long as the written directive or notes of an oral directive clearly fitted the circumstances which prevailed at the time, the instructions ought to be respected. This is certainly an area of law where, if the practitioner has sufficient time, advice should be sought from the Trust Litigation Manager or a Defence Union if at all possible.

Remedies

The carrying out of any medical procedure without valid consent is a battery. Battery can be dealt with by the courts both as a crime and as a tort.

A patient could also sue in the tort of negligence if he could establish that the standard adopted by the doctor in, for instance, providing information, fell below that of a reasonably competent doctor at that time.

References

1   Donaghue -v- Stephenson, 1932 AC 562.
2   Palmer -v- Tees Health Authority & Hartlepool & East Durham NHS Trust, [1999] Lloyd's Rep Med 351.
3   McLoughlin -v- O'Brian, [1983] 1 AC 410.
4   Powell -v- Boladz, [1998] Lloyd's Rep Med 116.
5   M V Calderdale -v- Kirklees Heath Authority, [1998] Lloyd's Rep Med157.
6   Gold -v- Haringey Health Authority [1988] QB 481 (CA).
7   Bolam -v- Friem Hospital Management Committee, [1957] 1 WLR 582.
8   Capital Counties plc v Hampshire CC [1997] 2 All ER 865.
9   Bamett -v- Chelsea & Kensington Hospital Management Committee, [1969 1 QB 428.
10 Bolam -v- Friem Hospital Management Committee, [1957] 1 WLR 582.
11 Hunter -v- Hanley, 1955 SLT 213.
12 Bolitho -v- City & Hackney Health Authority, 1998 Lloyd's Rep Med 26.
13 Roe -v- Minister of Health [1954] 2 QB 66 (CA).
14 Bull -v- Devon Area Health Authority [1993] 4 Med LR 117.
15 Bamett -v- Chelsea & Kensington Hospital Management Committee, [1969] 1 QB 428.
16 Bonnington Castings Ltd -v- Wardlaw, 1956 AC 613.
17 Wilshire -v- Essex Area Health Authority [1988] AC 1074.
18 Bolitho -v- City & Hackney Health Authority, 1998 Lloyd's Rep Med.
19 Hotson -v- East Berks Area Health Authority, 1987 AC 750.
20 Brahams D. Ulna nerve injury after general anaesthesia and intravenous infusion. The Lancent 1984; 1: 1306.
21 Owens -v Liverpool Corporation, 1939 1KB 394.
22 Emeh -v- Kensington & Chelsea & Westminster Area Health Authority [1985] 2 WLR 233 (CA).
23 Crossman -v- Stewart [1977] 5 CCLT 45.
24 Judicial Studies Board Guidelines on General Damages, 2001, Blackstone Press.
25 Heil -v- Rankin 2000 Lloyd's Rep Med 203 (CA).
26 Wells -v- Wells [1999] AC 345.
27 Re MB (1997) 38 BMLR 175 (CA).
28 Freeman -v- Home Office (No 2) [1984] QB 524.
29 Appleton -v- Garrett (1995) 34 BMLR 23 (QBD).
30 Sidaway -v- Board of Governors of the Bethlem Royal Hospital and the Maudsley Hospital [1985] AC 871.
31 Sidaway -v- Board of Governors of the Bethlem Royal Hospital and the Maudsley Hospital [1985] AC 871.
32 Pearce -v- United Bristol Healthcare NHS Trust (1998) 48 BMLR 118 (CA).
33 Re F [1990] 2 AC 1.
34 Airedale NHS Trust -v- Bland [1993] 1 All ER 821 (HL).
35 Gillick -v- West Norfolk & Wisbech Area Health Authority [1986] AC 112.
36 Re T [1992] All ER: 649.
37 Re: C (Refusal of Medical Treatment) [1994] 1 FLR 31.

3

Non-litigious complaints procedures

I will lift up mine eyes unto the hills from whence cometh my help.

Psalms 121

Introduction

A patient's first port of call with any complaint is to the health care staff responsible for his treatment. The new NHS Guide which replaces the Patients' Charter (http://www.nhs.uk/nhsguide/) states, 'If you have particular concerns, you should speak to someone involved in your care first (such as a doctor, nurse, receptionist, or practice manager). In many cases it should be possible to sort out the problem straight away.'

It goes without saying that no matter how onerous or impossible it seems, the response to that first approach should be prompt and courteous. This can be difficult, of course. Staff in an accident and emergency department faced with an angry patient fuelled by a mixture of injury and alcohol can be forgiven for taking a different approach from that used by staff in the out-patient clinic.

If that first approach fails to satisfy the patient's needs the conversation often ends thus, 'You'll be hearing from my Solicitor'. Interestingly, patients often give oral warning to their doctors that they are going to seek a remedy through the courts. Using phrases such as 'solicitor' and 'court' is a way that patients use to express their anger. They may want to cause alarm or at least get some sort of response even though litigation often fails to provide the very thing that the patient seeks, namely an admission of fault, an explanation or an apology. As we saw in Chapter 1, the Department of Health does not currently allow a patient to seek legal redress whilst any internal complaints procedure is in operation.

The new patient advocacy and liaison services (PALS) which are being set up to act for patients and try to sort out any problems straight away are still in their infancy. By April 2002, a patient advocacy and liaison service should be available in all English NHS and primary care trusts. It is too early to know what effect these will have on complaints. An initial challenge will be to define the boundaries between PALS and the NHS Complaints Procedure.

NHS complaints procedure

At first sight, the NHS Complaints Procedure seems to be a well-intentioned and comprehensive scheme. However, in many cases, it fails to deliver. This is regrettable because, for the moment at least, it offers the best hope a patient has of getting either an explanation or an apology. Before considering the failings of the Procedure, we shall look at how it works and how a practitioner should deal with it.

The current NHS Complaints Procedure was introduced in 1996. There is official guidance[1] on how the procedure should work but there is also flexibility for local adaptation. The guidance sets out the requirements in respect of time limits, publicity, designated complaints managers, the role of the Community Health Councils and the establishment of a process for local resolution and the convening of an independent review panel.

Local resolution

This is a comprehensive entity designed to investigate and resolve complaints at the 'front line'. Health authorities, Trusts and primary care practices must appoint a complaints manager, respond to all complaints, reply to written complaints within a set time and publicise their arrangements. Unfortunately the initial investigation is often inadequate. This is, to say the least, unfortunate, as the Medical Defence Union considers that properly handled, local resolution can resolve around 75% of grievances.

Oral complaint

This is often the first indication of dissatisfaction and, in hospital, is usually made to both nursing and medical staff. It must be taken seriously. A frequent difficulty is dissecting out the important issues within the complaint. How often does a patient complain with equal intensity about, for example, a wound infection and the fact that yesterday's food was cold? Almost every practitioner will also be familiar with the 'relative visiting from abroad' scenario. A daughter, say, flies in from California having not seen her mother for 3 or 4 years, finds her at death's door, and riddled with guilt lambasts everyone in sight. It is not easy to stay cool and deal with what could be a well-founded complaint. Another increasingly common problem is that many patients couch their complaint in threatening terms. Health care staff have little defence against this and many find it very demoralising. Failing to address this sort of problem may be as much to blame for difficulties in staff recruitment as more obvious reasons such as the modest salaries found in the health care sector.

Lack of time is another serious difficulty. In a packed day on a very tight schedule, prioritising work along the way, the decision to deal with clinical work rather than spend significant time with relatives seems justified. The hub of the problem is that most clinicians do not have time built into their work schedules to deal with complaints in the way that patients now expect. For most clinicians, dealing with a complaint either orally or in writing, is an extra task that must somehow be shoe-horned into an over-busy day. If, as now seems to be the case, there is to be an even greater role for front line health care workers in dealing with complaints, then, to be effective, protected time must be provided.

Despite these difficulties, try to give complainants as much time as you can possibly afford and focus on defining the issues. It is most important that a complainant feels that their complaint has been taken seriously and that, if appropriate, action has been taken to improve the service. An apology for what has happened is not an admission of liability. Only too often, patients end up in a solicitor's office saying, 'no-one would talk to me' . . . 'I'm only here because I don't want this to happen to someone else and no-one would listen to me.'

Not uncommonly, the problem lies in a breakdown of communication between the patient/relative and health care staff. Whilst this can often be the fault of the patient/relative, health care staff should develop expertise in preventing such a breakdown occurring. This is easier said than done but, without doubt, skills in this area would reduce the lawyers' workload.

Most health care workers make it a routine to record oral complaints in the relevant patient's records. This is good practice. Apart from the date and time, it is useful to record who was present, a brief description of the problem and a brief description of your response. If further action is taken as a result, this should be recorded as well. Though not routinely done, is there any harm in asking the complainant to countersign your entry? This sends out a message that the complaint is being taken seriously and that you are anxious to get to the heart of the matter. It might also deter the serial frivolous complainer who may one day cry wolf too often despite everyone's best intentions.

Suggested procedure for oral complaints:

* make time
* listen
* explain
* apologise if necessary
* record.

Written complaints

These are familiar to almost every clinician. They can be short and polite, long and rambling, frankly insulting, threatening or untrue. Whilst many a clinician would wish otherwise, parties and witnesses involved in a complaint to the proper authorities cannot be sued for defamation. Even if it turns out that what was said was untrue and derogatory, unless you can show that the defaming party was actuated by malice, they are protected by qualified privilege.

All written complaints must receive a response from the Chief Executive of the Trust. The guideline time limit for this response is 20 working days, i.e. a month. If the matter concerns clinical issues, the defence organisations will help practitioners in general or private practice formulate a response. The defence organisations are only relevant in relation to general or private practice; they have no locus in the hospital complaints procedure. Obviously, to be effective, a draft response should be sent to them at the earliest opportunity. It is a good idea to ask to see the 'official' letter before it goes out. It is not unknown for a complaints manager to 'interpret' a clinician's response inappropriately and this should be remedied if your clinical judgement is at issue.

The usual advice is to make an apology at this point. It can be difficult to get this right. On the one hand, sometimes the apology is so fulsome that the complainant becomes convinced there must have been negligence. In other cases, it is rather off-hand and leads to further grievance.

Whilst there is no right way to compose a response, there are several points to bear in mind. Perhaps the most important point is to keep your own copy of the draft you send to your complaints manager. The final letter sent by your Chief Executive should contain the substance of your response but, even if accurate, it may not contain all of the facts that you consider relevant. If the matter comes before the court, relevant documents will be disclosed. There may be matters covered in your original response that will be in your favour should you find yourself facing a judge.

A difficulty encountered by many front line staff is that their complaints manager waters down their factual response to the complaint. Complaints managers prefer to write positive letters and to avoid contention. Part of this is due to a belief that an 'oil on troubled water' style is more likely to defuse a complaint. Partly it may be due to the fact that many complaints managers have not received appropriate training for their job and do not have the necessary legal skills to allow them to take a more proactive line. Compare the average letter sent out by a hospital with that sent by, say, an insurance company.

Hopefully, the whole complaints system will be radically restructured soon but until that time, the sensible approach is to draft the letter of response that you would like sent and keep a copy.

The draft should include a chronology of events. So often a patient's complaint of e.g. a missed diagnosis is focussed on their immediate history. In the context of previous years of medical history, your actions, which at first sight appear incompetent, may have been very reasonable. An example will be the patient who presents with a similar history to an illness suffered 12 months earlier. Thorough investigations at that time may have been negative leading to a less proactive approach at the second presentation. This may not have been the correct approach but is more reasonable than if you had failed to investigate at all.

Another problem arises when patients refuse investigations or treatment, then change their mind and complain they should have been treated earlier. It can seem like a no-win situation. All that can be done is to thoroughly document all of the facts and all of your reasons at each stage of management.

These are letters that you must not put off writing. Unpleasant a task though it is, putting your actions and reasons down on paper can be helpful and remind you that your reasoning was sensible even if the outcome was not what you or the patient would have wished.

Written response to a complaint

Don't delay
Be transparent and accurate
Keep a copy of your own draft reply
Include a chronology of events
Document the reasons for your actions
Ask to see the letter sent out by the Chief Executive.

Generally speaking, health care staff give more of themselves emotionally than other workers in service industries and are therefore much more vulnerable to criticism. Despite this, there is still very little help available. Remember also, that we live in a consumer society. It is part of our culture now to believe that change and improved service is achieved through complaint. Try very hard not to take complaints personally. If you can use a complaint to persuade management that you need more staff, equipment, time then so much the better.

If the complaint has highlighted a deficiency in your practice, take the opportunity to get help and put things right. The Lord Chief Justice, Lord Woolf has made it clear that the courts will interfere where doctors have '... lost sight of the limits on their power and authority.' And who act '... as though they were able to take any action they thought desirable irrespective of the views of others.' It may be optimistic to suggest that complaints can be a learning opportunity but, if the staff concerned have appropriate feedback, complaints could have a positive effect on quality assurance.

Finally, when composing your draft response keep in mind three points. Most complainants assume that there will be some degree of cover-up and need to be actively persuaded that this is not so. The best way to achieve this is through transparency and factual accuracy. Secondly, most complainants want to talk face to face with someone from the front line of care and it is never too late to offer this opportunity even if earlier encounters were unsatisfactory. Thirdly, talking to complainants and writing letters is time-consuming but the time taken pales into insignificance when compared with the hours of lost sleep and time involved in both an Independent Review Panel review and a court case.

Independent review panel

If the complainant, or their carer or relative, is not satisfied with the local resolution outcome, then they can request that an Independent Review Panel (IRP) considers their complaint. When they make this request, a convener, who is often a non-executive, non-clinical director of the Trust will decide whether an IRP review should take place. The convenor can take clinical advice from the Trust's medical director or from an independent practitioner in the relevant specialty chosen from a list held regionally.

There is no automatic right to a review. Much has been written about the fairness and impartiality of such a system. Without doubt, it is the Achilles' heel of the NHS

Complaints Procedure. Of particular note, there will not be an IRP review if legal proceedings are pending or threatened.

A practitioner should be told of any request by a complainant for an IRP but does not have the right to put his case to the convener or to appeal any decision to establish an IRP.

If the convenor decides against an IRP, the complainant can then go to the Health Service Commissioner (Ombudsman).

The panel

- The convenor who dealt with the IRP request
- An independent lay chairperson (nominated by the regional office of the NHS executive)
- An independent lay member (nominated by the regional office of the NHS executive)

If the complaint concerns clinical issues
- Two clinical assessors (from outside the relevant area; nominated by the regional office of the NHS executive)

The IRP is required to investigate those aspects of the complaint that remain unresolved following 'local resolution'. The convenor should have identified these in the decision letter sent to both the complainant and the practitioner.

Once its investigation is complete, the IRP should make a report in which it sets out its conclusions with comments and suggestions.

The Chairperson, with contributions from the other panel members, can decide how the investigation is conducted. The panel meeting is held in private.

If you are asked to attend a panel meeting you should go. Not to do so may put you in breach of contract. In any event, you need to know what is being said and to correct factual inaccuracies and you need to explain your actions.

What to do beforehand

- Read through everything you are going to take.
- Mark up relevant entries with sticky labels.
- Make a list of the questions you would ask if you were on the panel and think through your replies.
- Consider how you could prevent a similar incident happening again.

What to take

- All relevant correspondence
- All of the patient's medical records
- Any notes or relevant diary entries
- Pen and paper
- Tolerance.

Almost always, the complainant and the complained about are interviewed separately. The panel will ask questions and can interview anyone else whom it considers can provide relevant information.

When attending a panel meeting, both parties can take someone with them who may be allowed, if the Chairperson agrees, to speak to the panel. Legally qualified persons cannot act as an advocate on your behalf. If you want someone to accompany you, take a friendly doctor rather than a friendly lawyer.

Once the meetings have taken place, the panel may provide a draft report, which will be sent to everyone who addressed the meeting, to allow them to check for factual accuracy only. Note, however, that this is at the discretion of the Chairperson.

Having considered all of the evidence including all the previous written correspondence, the Chairperson draws up a final report. The report should include the findings of fact, the panel's opinion on the complaint bearing in mind the findings of fact, the panel's reasons for reaching that opinion. The panel's report should also include a signed report from the clinical assessors. If the panel has disagreed with any of the content of the assessors report, that too should be included along with the panel's reasons for that disagreement.

Finally, the panel can include any relevant suggestions on how the service could be improved as a result of its findings.

Generally speaking, the panel's report will be distributed to the following:

- The complainant
- The patient, if not the complainant
- The health care staff named in the complaint
- Any other person interviewed by the panel
- The panel members
- The clinical assessors
- Regional Director of Performance Management (or equivalent)
- Health Authority Chief Executive
- Health Authority Chairman.

The Chairperson can withhold any part of the report in the interests of confidentiality of a patient who is not a complainant or any third party. Part of the report can also be withheld if this is necessary in the interests of the health of the complainant or a patient who is not a complainant.

Once the Health Authority Board has considered the report, the Chief Executive will write to the complainant advising of any action that has been taken as a result. The panel investigation should be completed within 3 months of the date of request for an IRP review though this is not always the case. The panel is not allowed to suggest or recommend disciplinary action or referral of anyone to their professional regulatory body.

Undoubtedly, the most painful part of this procedure for front line health care staff is having their performance picked over by their peers. To the outsider, the complainant, there is a strong suspicion that peers are unlikely to find a colleague wanting. Clinical assessors can also find the task daunting and may suffer pangs of '. . . there but for the grace of God go I'. It is a system crying out for change – everyone suffers and there are few winners.

If the complainant is unhappy, their next step is to go to the Ombudsman though, in practice, the next step is usually a visit to a solicitor.

In order to see the system at work, consider the following case scenario but note that any resemblance to persons living or dead is purely coincidental.

Case history

Mrs J,   age 65,   smoker.

Sent to Acute Admissions Unit at St Somewhere's Hospital by her GP.

Admitted to general medical ward at 18:50 hours.

Presentation:	Central chest pain for several hours.
Previous history:	Recurrent central chest pain, worse at night and when bending over weeding garden, no positive relationship to exercise.
On Examination:	Overweight. No other abnormalities found.
Plan:	Primary investigations to exclude acute myocardial infarction (MI). Further investigations as an outpatient to look for evidence of gastro-oesophageal reflux.
Results:	Blood tests normal – no evidence of acute MI. Electrocardiogram normal. Chest X-ray normal.
Outcome:	Sent home following Consultant ward round the following morning. Died suddenly at home later the same day. Post-mortem reveals severe coronary stenosis. Cause of death: myocardial infarction.
Complaint:	Son telephones and asks to speak to Consultant. Consultant replies by telephone and tells son that nothing else could have been done.

Son writes to complaints manager to say:

1. Mother was not admitted to the heart care unit even though the admitting doctor said they had to rule out a 'heart attack'.
2. Once her tests were completed and she had been admitted to the general ward, mother did not see a doctor until the next morning.
3. No-one spoke to the family before mother discharged.

Complaints manager sends copy of son's letter to Consultant and asks him to reply within 14 days.

Consultant replies within 14 days with an account of the history, examination findings and results of investigations. States that nothing more could have been done and apologises that no one spoke to family before Mrs J was discharged.

Son not happy that his specific grievances have been answered and requests an independent review.

Convenor agrees to hold an IRP review and requests reports from two (relevant) clinical assessors.

Both assessors write positive reports save that communication could have been better.

Son remains unhappy. Considers there has been an internal cover-up. Local newspaper carries stories of patients being discharged early due to lack of beds.

Son visits solicitor.

Case eventually abandoned.

Moral: This is the sort of complaint that could probably have been resolved by better Local Resolution. Where communication is an issue, it is a good idea to ensure that any future communication is as good as possible. A face-to-face discussion may have achieved more than a telephone discussion.

The points raised by the son should have been specifically answered even if the treating Consultant considers them irrelevant to the care that was provided.

Health service commissioner

The Health Service Commissioner is now allowed to consider clinical matters and complaints relating to primary care as well as grievances about the complaints process itself. Less well-known is that practitioners have access to the Ombudsman if they have suffered hardship or injustice because of the complaints process. The Ombudsman will see all of the letters and reports from local resolution and the IRP review. He can ask for further independent advice before interviewing all of those involved.

Preparation for this interview should be much the same as preparation undertaken for the IRP review. A practitioner can take a professional 'friend'. This is a good idea. In much the same way that friends accompanying patients hear more of what the doctor has to say, so the 'friend' at Ombudsman's review is much more likely to pick up details that you may miss.

Help is also available to general practitioners and private practitioners from Defence Organisation advisors. Even if you are convinced of the merits of your case, it can be useful to talk matters through.

The Ombudsman will prepare a draft report. If you need to correct any error of fact, take any help available from your Defence Organisation.

The final report is circulated to the same parties as the IRP review report. The main difference is that the Ombudsman will address questions of fault and can make a recommendation about disciplinary action or reference to the appropriate regulatory body.

Criticisms of the complaints procedure

Many patients tell us that they are deeply unhappy with the complaints procedure and cite it as a reason for seeking redress through the courts. Our experience is borne out by evidence given to the House of Commons Select Committee on Health by the Consumers' Association.[2] In 1997, the Consumers' Association carried out a survey of patients who had complained. They found that over 40% of respondents were unhappy with the overall way that their complaint had been handled. Arguably, those who respond to such a survey are perhaps more likely to be those who were unhappy. Equally worrying, more than a third of respondents did not consider that appropriate action was taken to prevent their problem from happening again.

The Public Law project also gave evidence to the Select Committee. They found that:

- The initial investigation of the complaint was often poor.
- The convener was not seen as independent.
- The convener and the IRP chairperson were uncertain of their roles.
- There was a lack of consistency between different areas.
- There was a lack of training for complaint handlers.
- There was too little external monitoring, and it was therefore unclear how well complaints were reviewed and whether action was taken by GPs or Trusts.

The main criticism from consumers is the apparent lack of impartiality and transparency. The main criticism from health care staff is that they receive very little support from management in dealing with aggressive and ill-founded complaints.

In its NHS Guide, the Government has stated that it '. . . is evaluating the complaints procedure. The Government will act on the outcome of this evaluation and reform the complaints procedure to make it more independent and meet patients' needs.' It would perhaps be helpful for morale within the NHS, if the Government also recognised the needs of front line staff.

Disciplinary procedures

Whilst the IRP cannot recommend disciplinary action, the Chief Executive of the Trust, after considering the IRP report, can decide to take matters further. Generally speaking, this step will be taken if it is thought in the best interests of patients and of the service generally. Patients have no say in this decision. The employer has to decide whether it is in the interests of patient safety or in the interests of the doctor themselves to suspend a practitioner during any investigation into misconduct, whether professional or personal. A few years ago, the medical press carried critical articles on the fate of doctors suspended whilst awaiting further investigations. This pointed up the fact that some doctors, later vindicated, had been suspended for several years at a considerable cost to themselves and to the NHS. In response, the Secretary of State for Health ordered a review of current suspension procedures and published 'Supporting doctors, protecting patients. A consultation paper on preventing, recognising and dealing with poor clinical performance of doctors in the NHS in England'.

Having completed the consultation process, in April 2001, the Government set up a new, national advisory body, the National Clinical Assessment Authority (http://www.ncaa.nhs.uk), to provide better protection for patients and support for doctors (see Chapter 1). The NCAA describes its general role as dealing with concerns about doctors in difficulty by providing advice, taking referrals and carrying out targeted assessments where necessary. Interested readers are advised to visit the NCAA website for more details.

Regulatory bodies

There are various regulatory bodies for the different health care sector workers. Relevant addresses and web sites are set out in Appendix 4.

The GMC's remit is to protect patients, provide guidance to doctors, set standards for medical practice and maintain a register of medical practitioners. It has statutory powers to take action when a doctor is convicted of a criminal offence, of serious professional misconduct, seriously deficient performance or unfitness to practice through ill-health.

Unfortunately, in its present format, the GMC is failing to convince the public that it is effectively managing these roles. To some extent this is unfair, as the GMC has made significant progress in recent years in certain areas. Any practitioner wishing to avoid successful legal proceedings should study and adhere to the advice offered in the GMC booklets on standards of medical practice.

The sustained criticism directed at the GMC has led to a major review. The resulting anticipated wide-ranging re-organisation includes governance proposals, more patient involvement, revalidation and 'Fitness to Practice' reforms and are likely to receive Government support.

Criminal offences

Police involvement is not the rarity it once was and if any criminal proceedings are taken against a doctor, these override any other complaints procedures. There have been a few high profile cases in recent years that have driven the public to question the profession's insistence on self-regulation. Should you, dear reader, find yourself the subject of GMC proceedings, or worse, police enquiries, then you must immediately seek professional help.

Alternatives to litigation

'Package' approach

If, after investigation, it is decided that a complaint is well founded, is there anything else the Trust can do other than write to the complainant to explain and apologise? In its report, the National Audit Office[3] recommended that patients should be offered a wider range of non-financial remedies to resolve small and medium-sized claims. This 'package' approach allows claims managers to offer other remedies as well as some financial compensation. The NAO found evidence that this approach could be successful and quoted case studies in their report such as:

- A 4-week course of psychological counselling for a woman left awake for 5 minutes during a hysterectomy, plus £5000.
- Fast access to remedial surgery for a teacher following negligent damage to an arm along with a taxi to hospital, childcare whilst an in-patient and early morning physiotherapy sessions so that no work was lost.

Mediation

Despite a pilot study,[4] mediation has not found favour in clinical disputes to the same extent that it has been adopted in other areas of law. It is defined as a private process, which seeks to maximise the parties' interests and can take into account remedies not capable of being granted by the courts. The power to agree a solution is with the parties. Whilst there is a neutral third party present to facilitate the negotiation, this mediator cannot impose a solution.

The NAO found that only 2% of Trusts usually offer mediation. This despite the fact that the Litigation Authority representing Trusts has required its solicitors handling claims to offer mediation wherever appropriate.

Advantages of mediation:

- less adversarial
- in tune with Government guidance
- more creative and relevant remedies can be offered
- without prejudice.

Disadvantages of mediation:

- inappropriate where damages likely to be high
- inappropriate where the point at issue is a point of law
- no incentive to mediate if either party believes its case is strong
- not necessarily cheap.

Other sources of information

Unless discouraged by local policy, a potentially difficult situation can sometimes be defused by offering the aggrieved party information on sources of independent advice. Community Health Councils (CHC) which traditionally filled this role are now being replaced by PALS (see above) except in Wales. Abolition of the CHCs has not been welcomed in all quarters, as an initial perception is that the PALS based in each NHS Trust will lack their independence.

Patient groups, which have continued to flourish since the advent of the Internet, can offer a sympathetic ear and advice on realistic outcomes of treatment. Many hospital departments and general practice surgeries do put out leaflets and telephone numbers of reputable organisations. There is no point hoping that patients and their relatives will not look for advice elsewhere so it as well to be proactive.

Action for Victims of Medical Accidents (AVMA) is a very well-regarded organisation that has been at the forefront of reform. AVMA tends to strike a chill in medical hearts but the Government has adopted many of its campaign initiatives. AVMA has drawn attention to the need for the collection of statistics, the understanding of the causes of accidents, the impact of accidents on patients and their families and the need for a change in culture.

Defence Societies have always been and remain a general practitioner's main source of support when complaints fall on their desks. They offer advice by telephone and should be consulted earlier rather than later. Whether any of the newly created and proposed organisations will also offer support at the front line remains to be seen.

The future

The Lord Chancellor has said that government departments will only go to court as a last resort and that they will settle cases by alternative dispute resolution whenever the other side agrees to it. In practice, there is little evidence of this so far.

The 'package' approach where complaints managers work with patients to offer suitable, relevant and acceptable levels of compensation before lawyers get involved must be an attractive way forward. On the other hand, complaints managers need the relevant training and skills.

There is a real fear amongst front line health care staff that unworthy complainants are compensated as a 'cheap option' and that unmeritorious cases are not defended with rigor unless it is cost-effective so to do. This concern is seldom addressed. It would appear that GPs who have more control over legal proceedings, are in a much stronger position to defend their honour than hospital staff.

References

1   Complaints – listening...acting...improving: Guidance on implementation of the NHS complaints procedure, DoH, 1996.
2   Sixth Report of the House of Commons Select Committee on Health: procedures relating to adverse clinical incidents and outcomes in medical care. London: HMSO, 1999.
3   National Audit Office. Handling clinical negligence claims in England. Report by the Comptroller and Auditor General HC 403 Session 2000–2001: 3 May 2001. The Stationery Office, London.
4   Mediating medical negligence claims: an option for the future? Mulcahy, London: The Stationery Office, 2000.

4

Anatomy of a claim

Agree with thine adversary quickly whiles thou art in the way with him; lest at any time the adversary deliver thee to the judge and the judge deliver thee to the officer, and thou be cast into prison. Verily I say unto thee, thou shalt by no means come out thence, till thou hast paid the uttermost farthing.

St Matthew 5:25–26

Introduction

Most patients who, for whatever reason, become dissatisfied with the outcome of treatment complain directly to the appropriate health care provider. This usually means that either the hospital or GP practice complaints procedure will be followed allowing the matter to be dealt with swiftly and, in many cases, to the satisfaction of all concerned. Occasionally, however, the first you will know of the existence of a problem is a formal request for the release of the notes. This request may come either from the patient themselves or via a solicitor. Such requests can never be ignored, and are, undoubtedly, best dealt with expeditiously and, in any event, within the relevant time limit.

Voluntary disclosure of medical notes

There are various statutory provisions governing a patient's rights to see and obtain copies of their notes, and these are considered in detail shortly. However, don't forget that the notes can be released to the patient on a voluntary basis, with the minimum of formality. Many patients who are dissatisfied with medical treatment received by them (or often a deceased relative) and who visit a solicitor for advice, frequently express the desire simply to obtain an explanation as to what, if anything, went wrong.

Time invested at the outset, taking the patient (or relative) through the notes, explaining the procedures, treatments and attendant risks may well prove to be effective in allaying the suspicions of the patient by demonstrating that not all undesirable outcomes have their origins in substandard treatment. If Uncle Fred was going to die anyway, and proceeded to do so despite your heroic efforts, you will do little harm by explaining this fact (gently) to his nearest and dearest. You may find that this informal approach prevents the clinical relationship from deteriorating any further and, perhaps more importantly, may even prevent further costs to the practice or Trust and professional embarrassment to the doctor or other health care workers involved.

Having said all that, caution should be exercised if there is any possibility that a valid claim may exist. If that is the case, you should certainly seek the advice of your Defence Organisation, if you are a member, or the Trust litigation or risk manager before embarking on such a course of action. Remember, that any admission you make could be used against you in any subsequent court action, and will certainly harm your popularity with those trying to defend your actions.

Statutory provisions for disclosure of medical notes

The relevant law, as it relates to England and Wales, is primarily contained in the Access to Medical Reports Act 1988, The Access to Health Records Act 1990 and The Data Protection Act 1998 and regulations made under the provisions of this Act. Different legislative regimens cover the situation in Northern Ireland and Scotland. We will begin by considering the most straightforward Act first, The Access to Medical Reports Act.

Access to Medical Reports Act 1988

The Access to Medical Reports Act regulates the rights of individuals to obtain access to medical reports about themselves provided by medical practitioners for employment or insurances purposes. It only applies to reports provided for these reasons. In deciding if a report is supplied for employment or insurance purposes, it is the purposes of the person or organisation commissioning the report which are to be considered.

Before any employer, prospective employer or insurance company requests a doctor to provide a report, they must first inform the individual who is to be the subject of the report that the request is to be made. This notification must be in writing and must inform the subject of their right to withhold consent to the preparation of the report.

The subject of the report also has two further rights of which they must be notified. These are, first, the right to see the report before it is submitted to the employer or insurance company and, second, to request the doctor to make amendments to the report to correct any parts which the subject considers to be inaccurate or misleading. If the doctor is prepared to accede to this request, the report should be amended accordingly. If the doctor is not prepared to accede in total or in part, the subject has the right to provide to the doctor a statement of the subject's views on the report and this statement must be attached to the report before it is submitted to the employer or insurance company.

Copies of the report supplied for the purposes of insurance or employment should be retained by the doctor for 6 months from the date upon which they are supplied. This is because the subject of the report can request to see the report or be supplied with a copy within that period. While, as a general rule, copies of the reports must be provided, the doctor is not obliged to provide any part of a report which would, in the opinion of the practitioner, be likely to cause serious harm to the physical or mental health of the subject or other person. The doctor is also allowed to withhold the parts of a report that would indicate the intentions of the practitioner to that subject. Parts of a report may also be withheld if they would be likely to reveal the identity of any person who provided information about the subject of the report unless that person consents or is a health care professional involved in the treatment of the subject and has provided information in that capacity. Where a copy of the report is requested and is given to the subject, the doctor may charge a reasonable fee for the provision of the report.

Access to Health Records Act 1990

The second piece of legislation of relevance is the Access to Health Records Act 1990. The Act has, to some extent, been amended and superseded by the Data Protection Act 1998, more of which later. The Access to Health Records Act created, for the first time, a right for patients to see their medical records. This is not, however, an unqualified right, conferring upon the doctor some discretion to withhold information where the doctor considers it is in the best interests of the patient that this information be withheld from them.

Sections 1 and 2 of the Act provide definitions of certain key matters such as: What constitutes a health record, who is the holder of such records and who is considered to be a "health professional" for the purposes of the Act? Health Professionals are listed as a:

a. registered medical practitioner
b. registered dentist
c. registered optician
d. registered pharmaceutical chemist
e. registered nurse, midwife or health visitor
f. registered chiropodist, dietician, occupational therapist, orthoptist or physiotherapist
g. registered osteopath
h. clinical psychologist, child psychotherapist or speech therapist
i. art or music therapist employed by health service body
j. scientist employed by such a body as head of a department.

Section 3 used to set out the classes of persons who were entitled to apply for records under the Act. However, since the coming into force of the Data Protection Act 1998 on 1 March 2000, the main categories of applicant, such as the patient themselves, a person acting on the persons behalf (e.g. a solicitor), a parent on behalf of their child or a person managing the affairs of one who is incapable, have been deleted. Now the only categories of applicant for access to notes under the Access to Health Records Act are the personal representatives of a patient who has died or any person who may have a claim arising out of the patient's death.

The Act sets out time limits for the provision of access to the notes. Where all of the notes concerned have been made within the 40 days proceeding the application, the time for the release of the notes is 21 days from the date of the application. Where, however, all or part of the notes concerned were made more than 40 days before the date of the application then the applicable period for the period for the provision of access to the notes is 40 days from the date of the application. If, as the holder of the records, you are of the view that an application does not contain sufficient information to enable you to identify the patient or to satisfy yourself that the applicant is entitled to make the application and within a period of 14 days beginning with the date of the application you request the applicant to furnish you with such further information as you may reasonably require to satisfy yourself of the above then the time limit for the provision of notes does not run until the further information, as requested by you, is supplied.

A further point worth noting is that there are cases where the right of access may be partly or wholly excluded. Examples of this were wider prior to the coming into force of the Data Protection Act but the remaining provisions are, nevertheless, of some significance. For instance, where an application is made for the provision of the records of a deceased patient, the records shall not be released if they contain a note made at the patient's request that he did not wish the notes to be released after his death. Similarly, notes shall not be released to an applicant where they contain information provided by the deceased in the expectation that it would not be disclosed to the applicant at some future date or, perhaps more likely in practice, information obtained as a result of any examination or investigation to which the patient consented in the expectation that the information would not be so disclosed. This may be particularly relevant in the case of testing for HIV or other sexually transmitted diseases. The health care provider is also under a duty not to provide any part of a record which, in the opinion of the record holder (i.e. you), would disclose any information not relevant to any claim which may arise out of the patient's death. The Act, as amended, also provides that access shall not be given to records if the release of information contained within those records is likely to cause serious harm to the physical or mental health of any individual or contains information relating to or provided by an individual other than the patient who could be identified from that information. Notes made before the commencement of the Act, i.e. 1 November 1991, are protected from disclosure under the Act.

It would certainly seem that the wording of the Act is such that health professionals should exercise caution in releasing the notes of a deceased patient, even to their relatives, where any of the above potential exclusions apply. The way in which the Act is phrased is such that 'access shall not be given' where the exceptions apply. Therefore, where the holder of the record is aware of these exceptions, disclosure is prohibited.

A further duty is placed upon a health service body holding records. This duty is created by Section 7 of the Act which requires that the health care professional with care of the patient at the time of the request or, if there are no present care arrangements in respect of that patient, the professionals who had care of that patient in the past should be consulted prior to the health service body forming an opinion as to whether or not they are satisfied as to any matter which they are required to consider by this Act. In other words, medical records managers must seek the opinion of the treating clinicians before they release any records.

Finally, the fees which health care professionals are now allowed to charge for the provision of notes under the Access to Health Records Act has been modified by the fees order made under the Data Protection Act 1998. This order, which came into force on 1 March 2000, provides that reasonable charges can be levied for the provision of copy notes but that those charges are limited to a maximum of £50.

Data Protection Act 1998

The majority of the provisions of the Data Protection Act 1998 came into force by order made by the Secretary of State on 1 March 2000. This Act is now the primary Act under which access to health records can be gained by patients. As discussed above, the provisions of this Act substantially amended the Access to Health Records Act which had, in practical terms, worked quite well. The new Act is, however, extremely complex and comprehensive in its coverage. It provides for numerous different situations most of which are not relevant for our present discussion. For the sake of brevity we will, therefore, deal only with the relevant sections.

Section 1 defines data. The definition is broad and, for our purposes, also includes data held within a 'relevant filing system'. The definition of a relevant filing system includes a system not necessarily held on computer but which is structured so that information dealing with individuals can be readily identified and is readily accessible. Data were further defined as to include information which forms part of an accessible record the definition of which is set out in Section 68. Section 68, for its part, confirms that a 'health record' is an 'accessible record' within the meaning of the Act and defines a 'health record' as a record which:

- consists of information relating to the physical or mental health or condition of an individual
  and
- has been made by or on behalf of a health professional in connection with the care of that individual.

Section 69 goes on to define health professional and, in so doing, provides a list very similar to that set out in the Access to Health Records Act, referred to above. Having established that health records come within the ambit of the Act, we now need to consider the rights of access to the notes all patients can exercise. The principle right of significance to medical practice is contained in Section 7 and is:

> *To have communicated to him in an intelligible form*
> *(i) The information constituting any personal data of which that individual is the data subject and*
> *(ii) Any information available to the Data Controller as to the source of those data.*

Section 8 goes onto augment this right by adding that in fulfilling a request to provide data of this sort, the patient should be provided with a copy of the information in a permanent form unless doing so is not possible or would involve disproportionate effort or, alternatively, the patient agrees not to have a copy. Significantly, the Act then goes on to place an additional burden on health care providers in that it states that, where any of the information provided is expressed in terms that are not intelligible without explanation, the copy notes must be accompanied by an explanation of those terms. The implications are, of course, crystal clear. Your notes consist of technical jargon and a set of symbols and squiggles which closely resemble a cross between Egyptian hieroglyphics and Babylonian cuniform. Your patient is entitled to have that explained to them, in writing: a time-consuming and thankless task.

You do not, however, need to provide access to notes unless the request is

- made in writing
- accompanied by the appropriate fee
- you have sufficient information to identify the information in question and satisfy yourself of the identity of the person making the request.

It is also not necessary to fulfil such a request where a previous request has been complied with unless a reasonable time has elapsed since that previous request. You are also not obliged to provide copy notes where so doing would reveal the identity of a third party from the notes unless the third party has consented or it is reasonable in all circumstances to comply with a request without the consent of the other individual, for example in releasing notes relating to the birth of a child, the mother can be clearly identified (and vice versa) but it would be unreasonable to withhold the notes on that basis as, in the vast majority of cases, the individuals concerned would know each other in any event.

Where the notes are to be released, the Act stipulates that release should occur within 40 days of a valid request being received. As previously stated, a valid request is one that provides sufficient details to identify the person making the request, the information sought and the fee. The Secretary of State has provided by Statutory Instrument, which came into effect on 23 October 2001, that the maximum fee for the provision of copy medical records is now £50. This will, no doubt, cause some consternation, particularly in the corridors of the finance departments of NHS Trusts. The patients have an argument, at the time of writing untested, that all information should be provided for the £50 fee. It is almost certain that items such as copy MRI scans, CT scans and ultrasound scans which are stored as computer data must be provided within the £50 fee. This was certainly not the case under the old regimen where, in some instances, Trusts were charging hundreds of pounds for copy scans. Those days are gone.

Under the new regimen, there continues to be a discretion on the part of the doctor to withhold all or part of any record where he considers that releasing the information would not be in the best interests of the patient. This is found in the Data Protection (Subject Access Modification)(Health) Order 2000. The exemptions from subject access rights occurs in two situations:

1. Where permitting access to the data would be likely to cause serious harm to the physical or mental health or condition of the data subject or any other person (which may include a health professional).

2. Where the request for access is made on behalf of another data subject, access can be refused if the data subject had either provided the information in the expectation it would not be disclosed to the applicant or had indicated that it should not be disclosed, or the data was obtained as a result of any examination or investigation to which the data subject consented on the basis that the information would not be disclosed.

Supreme Court Act 1981

Finally, and briefly, mention must be made of the provisions of Sections 33 and 34 of the Supreme Court Act 1981. Section 33 empowers the High Court to order a potential party to an action to produce copies of documents which they have in their possession before the proposed case commences, while Section 34 contains similar powers allowing the court to order the production of documents and other items held by persons who are not and will not be parties to an action. Since the advent of greater access by patients to their notes and records, the use of these measures has, fortunately, declined.

If your patient is intent on bringing a claim against you, the request for the notes is the first step in what can be a long and tortuous process. Despite the apparent lack of activity that will occur after the copy notes have been provided, your patient or, more likely their legal representatives, will be hard at work building the case against you. The focus of these efforts will be obtaining expert evidence which is the lynch pin of any clinical negligence claim. It would, therefore, now seem sensible to consider the role of an expert.

Expert witnesses

The purpose of this section is to set out, briefly, the role of the expert witness in a clinical negligence context. It is not intended to provide advice or guidance to those readers who propose to act as an expert witness in their own right. Anyone embarking on such a course, particularly for the first time, would be well advised to invest in a text directed to the topic such as *Medical Evidence*.[1]

A person is only competent to be called to give evidence as an expert if, in the opinion of the judge, he is properly qualified in the subject requiring expertise. Such expertise may be gained by academic qualification, training or experience. For instance, in *R -v- Oakley*,[2] a police officer who had appropriate qualifications and experience in accident investigation was allowed to give evidence as to how a road accident occurred. Similarly, in *R -v- Silverlock*,[3] the court held that a solicitor who had studied handwriting for 10 years, largely as a hobby, had properly been allowed to give his opinion as to whether the disputed handwriting was that of the accused.

Generally speaking, it is for the court to determine facts and issues within its competence. However, expert evidence is clearly required where the subject matter of the dispute and, therefore, some of the issues between the parties are of a technical or specialist nature. The judge then, no matter how learned, has to rely on the knowledge and experience of others to guide him in the making of his decision. In medical cases, the need for such expert assistance is obvious. The court will almost certainly need assistance with such questions as:

- What is usual practice under a given set of circumstances?
- What is the likely effect, particularly to the patient, of an act or omission?
- The effect or efficacy of drugs or treatment.

This clearly places a high burden on anyone who is seeking to provide expert assistance to the court. Mr Justice Cresswell in the 'The Ikarian Reefer',[4] summarised the position by suggesting that an expert's evidence should be:

- presented independently to the court and uninfluenced as to form or content by the exigencies of litigation
- objective – it is not the position of the expert witness to seek to be an advocate for one of the parties
- based on all material facts known to the expert including those which detract from his opinion
- within his area of expertise – an expert should clearly state when he is straying outside his area of expertise
- properly researched. If a view was provisional then the expert should say so.

This has now been embodied within Part 35 of the Civil Procedure Rules, as discussed below.

In many cases, particularly where it is necessary for an expert to make reference to medical developments or the use or effect of drugs, external sources of information are required by an expert witness either as part of his research in reaching his opinions or to provide support to the conclusion to which he has ultimately reached. There was, in the past, some dispute as to whether such information constituted hearsay but it is now well settled that experts may properly rely on the published research of others. In *H - v- Schering Chemicals Limited*,[5] Bingham J said

> If an expert refers to the results of research published by a reputable authority in a reputable journal the court would, I think, ordinarily regard those results as supporting inferences fairly to be drawn from them, unless or until a different approach was shown to be proper.

Similarly, data from a reputable source, although unpublished, can be relied upon by an expert. In *R -v- Abadom*,[6] expert evidence was required as to the identity of glass found in the shoe of a man convicted of robbery. The expert in question relied on unpublished Home Office statistics to conclude that the glass in question had a refractive index which was relatively uncommon. Such a reference to these statistics, although unpublished, was held to be proper.

Any expert witness, be it for the claimant or defendant, may ultimately be tested in court. It is not, therefore, enough that they are the 'leading light' in their field. Other qualities are undoubtedly required. In practice, the choice of expert to defend your position is likely to be made by the solicitors advising the Trust or instructed by your defence union. However, it is worth noting the comments made by Stuart-Smith LJ in the case of *Loveday -v- Renton*,[7] where he set out ten attributes of an expert witness which the court will use in assessing the weight to be attributed to his opinion:

- eminence
- soundness of opinion
- internal consistency and logic
- precision and accuracy of thought
- response to searching and informed cross-examination
- ability to face up to logic and make concessions
- flexibility of mind and willingness to modify opinions
- freedom from bias
- independence of thought
- demeanour.

In other words, they must be pre-eminent in their field, have the analytical abilities of Sherlock Holmes and the wisdom of Solomon.

While the latter attributes cannot be legislated for, the basis upon which an expert should now approach his role has been set out in the Civil Procedure Rules 1998. These are the new rules brought into force to implement the 'Woolf Reforms' and, largely, replace the old County Court and High Court regimens.

Part 35 of the Civil Procedure Rules 1998 sets out the duties of an expert. If you are engaged in that capacity, you would be well advised to obtain a copy of Part 35 and the Practice Direction which goes with it. In essence, it would be fair to say that the comments of Mr Justice Creswell in 'The Ikarian Reefer', referred to above, have become embodied in the rules. It is now clear that an expert owes his first duty to the court and must be objective in providing his evidence and that this duty overrides any other duty he may feel towards those from whom he has received instructions and by whom he has been paid. In fact, experts must now sign a declaration contained within their report that they understand their duty to the court and that they have complied with this duty. There is no set wording for this declaration. There are, however, suggested models.[8] The expert must also confine himself only to matters which are within his expertise.

The court also now has powers to appoint a joint expert to act in advising the court. It is, however, the case that this is only likely to occur in practice in clinical negligence cases in a limited number of circumstances. In general, because of the need to obtain expert evidence prior to the commencement of court proceedings, it is likely that both parties will have at least their liability and causation experts instructed and will have obtained reports from them before the case itself actually commences. In clinical negligence cases, the expert has a dual role. His first involvement (unless appointed as a joint expert) will be to advise one of the parties as to the merits and strength of their case. This first advice does not form part of the expert's report for the purposes of the court. The formal report suitable for exchange with the other side is produced at a later stage.

The rules do, however, provide that where experts are instructed by both parties, the court can direct that the experts are to discuss the case with a view to narrowing the issues between them so that at any subsequent trial, the only issues which will be decided by the judge are those which the experts have not, at that stage, managed to agree upon. This arrangement has been criticised by many lawyers on the basis, that in effect, it can take the question of liability and/or causation away from the court. This is particularly so where one expert is of a much stronger character than the other and manages to persuade his counterpart that his position is wrong and, consequently, the party who has instructed that expert may well find that their case is severely damaged or destroyed following the experts meeting. Various suggestions have been made to counteract that problem, the primary one of which is that lawyers should be present during the meeting of experts which should take place only when a tightly worded agenda is available. The meeting may then be directed at answering the questions set out in the agenda. Guidance on the drafting of such agendas has been provided by the Clinical Disputes Forum which recommends that the questions discussed by the experts should be closed questions in that they admit a yes or no answer.[9]

The Civil Procedure Rules have brought about two further innovations in respect of expert witnesses. These are, first, that the parties have a right to put written questions to their opponent's experts and, second, that the experts instructed in the case can themselves approach the court for directions from the court as to how they should carry out their function as expert witness. The expert can make such a request independent of the party or lawyers who have instructed him and can even do so without giving notice to those instructing him. This point would seem to reinforce the position of the expert as an independent entity having a direct relationship with the court.

Legal process

When the patient and their lawyers have their expert advices to hand, they must then decide whether to sue or not. If they decide to go ahead, it is likely that the patient's lawyers would advise them to follow the clinical negligence protocol prior to issuing proceedings in court. The clinical negligence protocol (see Appendix 3) is intended to bring about an early resolution of clinical negligence disputes, hopefully in some cases, prior to the issue of proceedings. Essentially, the protocol envisages the claimant sending a detailed 'letter of claim' which sets out the basis of the alleged negligence of the proposed defendants. The letter should also include details of the claimant's present condition and prognosis and financial details such as to allow the defendants a reasonable opportunity of calculating the potential level of damages resulting from, for instance, loss of earnings. Ideally, the defendants would then be allowed a period of 3 months within which to investigate the claim prior to court proceedings commencing. If, following investigations, the defendants decide to admit all or part of the claim they then have an opportunity to make an offer of settlement which, if acceptable to the claimant, brings matters to an end. If, however, the defendant does not feel disposed to make an offer during the 3-month period then it is open to the claimant to issue proceedings in the normal way. In reality, only cases that are straightforward and of relatively low monetary value will be settled in this way. An example of such a case may be one where there is a claim brought by parents arising from the death of a child where the parents will, in most cases, be entitled only to £10,000 bereavement damages and the relevant funeral expenses. The majority of more complex cases will, as in the past, result in contested litigation.

The court process for handling contested litigation, particularly litigation as complex as clinical negligence cases, is, as you may suspect, far from straightforward. We propose, therefore, to deal only with the basic steps which need to be taken in the management of a reasonably standard claim.

The first stage in the commencement of proceedings in clinical negligence cases is to decide if the proceedings are to be issued in the High Court or the County Court. The rules provide that claims valued at less than £50,000 should be commenced in the County Court whereas, if a claim exceeds £50,000 in value, the claimant has a choice of venue between the County Court and the High Court. It has to be said that while the County Court has, in this respect, unlimited financial jurisdiction, if a matter is extremely complex and of high value it is usual to issue it in the High Court. In practical terms, for the day to day management of the case, it makes precious little difference where the claim is issued. However, if the matter is likely to go to trial, a High Court case will be heard by a High Court Judge or a designated Circuit Judge. The theory being, at the risk of upsetting Circuit Judges, the higher value, more complex cases, will be heard by a higher level of Judge. Assuming, for our purposes, that the matter is issued in the County Court, the process is extremely straightforward. A "claim form" is completed and filed at court with the appropriate fee. The fee is determined by a sliding scale based on the value of the claim, the scale being changed from time to time. Once issued, the claim form stops time running for limitation purposes (see chapter 2) and sets in motion the formal part of the case.

A claim form has to be served within 4 months of the date of issue and, in most cases, it is served on solicitors nominated by the NHS Trust or the doctor's defence union. Prior to service of a claim form it is necessary to be in possession of various other documents required to be served with the form. These are:

1. *The Particulars of Claim.* This is a document which sets out the claimant's case and, in particular, identifies the allegations of negligence being made against the defendant. It also links those allegations to the injury which the claimant alleges he has suffered.
2. *A Medical Report.* This report, in its minimum form, is required to set out the claimant's present condition and prognosis. It must also list all the injuries in respect of which the claimant seeks to recover damages. It need not, however, deal with matters of negligence or causation.
3. *Schedule of Special Damage.* This document sets out the basis of the claimant's financial losses which are caused by, for instance, a loss of earnings. While it is possible to set out in the schedule the damages sought in respect of pain and suffering, it is unusual so to do.

The claimant's solicitor arranges to serve the claim form on the defendant, or his solicitors, along with a response pack. This is a document which sets out the steps to be taken by the defendant in respect of the claim. The defendant, or his solicitors, will usually file an acknowledgement of service with the court confirming when he has been served. The defendant then has a period of 14 days from the date upon which he received the documents from the claimant or, if he has filed an acknowledgement of service, a period of 28 days from the date of which he received the documents from the claimant to file his defence.

It is possible for the defendants to obtain an extension of up to 56 days from the claimants for the time of filing of the defence. In practice, it is usual for experienced clinical negligence solicitors to agree such extensions. If a further extension is, however, required, then it is necessary to seek the permission of the court.

Once the defendant has filed his defence at the relevant County Court, a copy is sent to the claimant and both parties are supplied with what is known as an 'Allocation Questionnaire'.

The Civil Procedure Rules provide for three categories of claim which are, generally, delineated by the value and complexity of the subject matter of the claim. They are:

1. *Small claims*: claims valued at £5 000 or less, unless they include a claim for personal injuries where the value of the pain and suffering is more than £1000.
2. *Fast-track claims*: claims valued at more than £5000 (except personal injury and housing) but not more than £15 000.
3. *Multi-track claims*: claims valued at over £15 000.

The purpose of the allocation questionnaire is to provide information to the judge which will enable him to allocate the cases to the appropriate track. Due to their complexity, clinical negligence claims will almost invariably be allocated to the multi-track.

The parties are invited to forward to the court proposed directions dealing with the conduct of the action after it has been allocated to a track. As these directions are relatively standard, even in extremely complex cases, the best way to illustrate them would be to set out a typical set of directions and explain each one in turn.

Specimen order

As you will see from the specimen order at the end of this chapter, the court provides a reasonably strict timetable setting out, at the start, the dates by which it is expected that the various stages should be completed.

Taking each stage in turn, the disclosure referred to in points numbered 1 and 2 is the process whereby the parties provide to their opponents details of documents which they respectively hold and which are of relevance to the case. The rules provide that you are to disclose documents:

1. on which a party relies
2. which adversely effect his own case
3. which adversely effect another party's case
4. which support another party's case
5. other documents which a party is required to disclose by a relevant practice direction.

In practice, in clinical negligence cases, disclosure is limited on the part of the health care provider to copies of the relevant medical records (which have already been released in any event), copies of any protocols which apply to the treatment received by the patient and copies of any adverse incident reports which came into existence as a result of the difficulties experienced by the claimant. The claimant, for his part, will generally only disclose documents relating to his special damage, for instance payslips, accounts, or tax returns.

The directions then provide for the exchange of lay evidence and expert evidence. This is, obviously, a self-explanatory step. It is usual, wherever possible, for such exchanges to take place simultaneously. This is usually achieved by the lawyers agreeing to place their witness statements in the post on a specified date in order that the parties both receive them at the same time. The process is then repeated for the expert evidence. In so doing, each party is denied the advantage of seeing their opponents' evidence prior to having to release their own.

Following exchange of evidence, it is usual to have a meeting of experts as discussed above. The court, generally, then orders the experts to file at court a memorandum of their points of agreement and disagreement. Unless agreed in advance, the parties cannot rely on this memorandum at trial. However, it clearly assists the court in determining how far apart the experts are and, therefore, how hotly contested the expert evidence is likely to be. This has practical consequences in terms of the length of trial and also has bearing on the more thorny problem of finding a trial date when all the experts are available to attend. It is this latter problem which the 'listing questionnaires' are intended to alleviate. The idea is that the parties provide lists of dates when their experts are available/unavailable to attend trial and the court staff can, then, find an appropriate window. In practice, this is easier said than done.

The grand finale of the whole process is a trial, a position to be avoided if at all possible.

The reality of life is that only a very small percentage of clinical negligence claims actually end up at trial. Experienced lawyers and expert witnesses are usually more than capable of sorting out which party is likely to win after the evidence has been exchanged and an agreement is, therefore, usually forthcoming. Agreements can be aided along the way by the use of what is known as Part 36 of the Civil Procedure Rules. This particular Part allows either party at any stage before or after proceedings but before trial to make an offer to settle. Essentially, a party writes to the opponents saying that they wish to settle and sets out the terms of that offer. The opponent then has 21 days within which to decide whether they accept or reject that offer. If the offer is accepted then the terms of settlement are thereby decided. If, however, the offer is rejected then there are cost consequences if the rejecting party fails to do better at trial than the offer which was put to them. A well judged offer, by either party, can therefore bring considerable pressure to bear on the opponents.

Most experienced lawyers try, as best they can, to settle matters before a judge imposes a solution. It is often better to acknowledge that there is a litigation risk and reach settlement terms based on that acknowledgement than it is to go for the 'all or nothing' approach of taking a matter to trial. Never forget, after a trial 50% of the parties leave the court disappointed.

Specimen order

IN THE ANYWHERE COUNTY COURT   Claim No: 123456

BETWEEN:

IVOR PROBLEM

                                                Claimant

- and -

DR BURKE (1)
DR HARE (2)

                                                Defendants

DIRECTIONS ORDER

1. The case be allocated to Multi Track.

2. There be standard disclosure by lists on or before 2nd October 2001.

3. There be inspection of documents on or before 9th October 2001.

4. There be mutual exchange of the statements of Witnesses of Fact on or before 6th November 2001.

5. There be mutual simultaneous exchange of expert evidence as to liability and causation on or before 4th December 2001, such experts being limited to two per party.

6. The Defendant to serve a Counter Schedule of Special Damages on or before 8th January 2002.

7. The experts of like disciplines are to meet with a view to narrowing the issues between them not later than 4.00 p.m. on 31st January 2002.

8. The experts do file in court not later than 4.00 p.m. on 15th February 2002 a memorandum of the points of agreement and disagreement with reasons for such disagreements.

9. The parties are to file listing questionnaires at court not later than 4.00 p.m. on 28th February 2002.

10. A case management conference be held on the first open date after 15th March 2002 with a time estimate of 1 hour.

DATED this 15th August 2001.

Alternative dispute resolution

The Civil Procedure Rules encourage the parties to enter into negotiations or to follow alternative methods of resolution for disputes. Pilot schemes have been tried for clinical negligence cases but, it has to be said, that alternative dispute resolution does not, at the moment, play a major role in clinical negligence litigation. This position will, undoubtedly, change in the next couple of years.

References

1   Medical Evidence, Clements, R. V. *et al*, (2001) Royal Society of Medicine Press.
2   R -v- Oakley [1979] RTR 417.
3   R -v- Silverlock [1894] 2QB 766.
4   The Ikarian Reefer [1993] Lloyd's Reports 68: [1995] 1 Lloyd's Reports 455.
5   H -v- Schering Chemicals Limited [1983] 1 All ER 849.
6   R -v- Abadom [1983] I WLR 126.
7   Loveday -v- Renton [1990] 1 Med LR 117.
8   Clinical Risk Vol.5 No.3 May 1999 p.91.
9   Clinical Risk (2000) 6: 149–152.

5

Inquests

Come he slow, or come he fast, it is but Death who comes last.
Sir Walter Scott 1771–1832

Role of the coroner

Coroners are appointed to have jurisdiction over defined geographical areas. They are usually appointed by the Local Authority for the relevant area. Their remit is to investigate deaths within their jurisdiction which have been brought to their attention. The death itself need not have occurred within that area. The purpose of the coroner's investigation is limited to:

- The identity of the deceased
- How, when and where he came by his death
- Details of the death required for registration purposes.

It is not the purpose of a coroner's court to determine any questions of civil or criminal liability. That does not, however, prevent a legal representative, particularly those of the family of the deceased, from attempting to use the inquest as an information-gathering exercise with a view to a civil claim or as a forum for making a point, for instance where the deceased died in custody.

Although ancient in its origins, the role of the coroner is now regulated by statute. Coroners carry out their function as regulated by the Coroners Act 1988 and the Coroners Rules 1984. To hold office, coroners must be solicitors, barristers or registered medical practitioners of at least 5 years standing.

Referral to the coroner

It is open to anyone to refer a death to the coroner if they so wish. In practice, however, most referrals to the coroner come from doctors, the police and the Registrar of Births, Marriages and Deaths. It is only the Registrar of Births, Marriages and Deaths who has a legal obligation to refer a death to the coroner if it falls within certain statutory categories. These include:

- Where the deceased was not attended during his last illness by a registered medical practitioner.
- Where it has not been possible to obtain a duly completed certificate of cause of death.

- Where from the certificate it is apparent that the deceased was not seen by the certifying doctor either after death or within 14 days before death.
- Where the cause of death appears to be unknown.
- Whether death was unnatural or likely to have been caused by violence or neglect or by abortion.
- Whether death appears to have occurred during a surgical operation before recovery from an anaesthetic.
- Whether death appears to have been caused by industrial disease or poisoning.

While there is no legal obligation on an individual doctor to report a death to the coroner, it is clearly sensible if faced with a death which is likely to fall within the above criteria to pre-empt the registrar by notifying the coroner at the earliest opportunity. It is probably fair to say that if, as a doctor, you have any doubts as to whether a matter should be brought to the attention of the coroner or not, it is better to report a death unnecessarily than fail to report one where the coroner ultimately becomes involved.

Coroners investigation

In the performance of his duties, the coroner is usually assisted by the coroner's officer who is a police officer attached to the coroner's office. In carrying out an investigation into a death the coroner will often call for the medical records of the deceased and statements from the various health care professionals involved in looking after the deceased.

Where it is suspected that the death may be the result of a crime, the coroner will hand over the full investigation to the police until the criminal investigation is concluded or the Crown Prosecution Service have taken a firm decision not to prosecute.

As part of his investigation, the coroner can order a postmortem examination which will be carried out usually by a Home Office appointed pathologist.

The coroner has the power to subpoena witnesses to attend before his court. While it is common practice for the coroner to canvas the views of interested parties as to the identity of the witnesses selected, the final choice of witnesses rests with the coroner. The coroner's decision as to witnesses is often based on the written statements which the witness provides during the coroner's investigation.

The inquest

The inquest is the formal hearing during which the coroner investigates the circumstances surrounding the death of the deceased. Where an investigation is likely to be lengthy or where criminal charges are involved, an inquest is often opened for identification evidence and then adjourned.

In more straightforward cases the inquest will open with identification evidence and then continue with oral evidence being received from the witnesses. Each witness gives their evidence in turn and is then questioned first by the coroner and then by the representatives of the other interested parties. Most inquests proceed with the coroner sitting alone but the coroner does, however, have the right to sit with a jury. Under certain circumstances, the coroner is obliged to summon a jury which shall consist of not fewer than 7 and no more than 11 jurors. The coroner must sit with a jury where the death occurred:

- in prison or police custody
- by the actions of a police officer in the execution of his duty
- due to an accident, poisoning or disease
- where an Act of Parliament requires the coroner to investigate
- where there is a continued risk to the public.

Where a jury is involved, the coroner must sum up the evidence and direct the jury as to the points of law. The coroner must also outline to the jury the possible verdicts which they can return.

The verdict

The verdict of the inquest comprises

- deceased person's identity
- injury or disease causing death
- time, place and circumstances of the injury
- cause of death
- registration particulars.

The conclusion as to death is often referred to as 'the verdict' by the general public. Although their use is not compulsory, certain terms are recommended to be used when handing down the verdict. These include:

- death from natural causes
- industrial disease
- dependent or non-dependent abuse of drugs
- accident or misadventure
- suicide
- unlawful killing
- open verdict.

Apart from suicide and unlawful killing, the coroner (and/or his jury) must reach their decision upon a balance of probabilities. Where a verdict of suicide or unlawful killing is reached it must be based on proof beyond a reasonable doubt. An open verdict is handed down where the court is unable to reach any other conclusion.

Finally, confusion often arises as to the meaning of the term 'misadventure'. It is a term which should not, now, generally be in use but does, however, still appear in verdicts. It is a term intended to convey the fact that the death occurred as the unintended outcome of an intentional, lawful act. Its use does not indicate that anyone is blameworthy in the death.

Appendix 1

Glossary of legal terms

Balance of probabilities	More likely than not
Battery	Physical contact without consent
Burden of proof	The obligation to prove
Causation	Relationship between cause and effect
Competence	An ability to comprehend, retain, believe and weigh up information so as to arrive at a choice
CPR	Civil Proceedure Rules 1998
Damages	Financial compensation
Duty of care	Undertaking by a practitioner to provide medical services to a patient
Foreseeability	Act or omission that you can reasonably predict would injure persons directly affected by it
Issue of proceedings	The start of formal legal action in a civil case
Liability	A legal obligation
Limitation	Time limit during which proceedings should be issued
Negligence	Breach of the duty of care resulting in damage
Statutory	Relating to an Act of Parliament
Tort	A civil wrong
Vicarious liability	Liability of one person for the results of the actions of another

Appendix 2
Notable legal cases – case summaries

Case summaries

Airdale NHS Trust -v- Bland

House of Lords [1993] 1 All ER 821
Keywords: persistent vegetative state, withdrawal of treatment, best interests of patient, sanctity of life, withdrawal of feeding, declaration by the court.

FACTS

On 15 April 1989, Anthony David Bland, then aged 17 went to the Hillsborough football ground to support Liverpool Football Club. Mr Bland found himself in the centre of a crush of fellow supporters which led to his lungs being crushed and punctured so as he stopped breathing. While he was unable to breathe his brain was deprived of oxygen. This led to irreversible brain damage in the cerebral cortex, the area of the brain which deals with the senses, voluntary movement, pain and consciousness. His brain stem, however, suffered less damage. This is because the brain stem, which controls the body's 'automatic' functions such as breathing and a passage of food through the gut, is less sensitive to oxygen deprivation. Mr Bland was, therefore, left in the position where, while his body was alive in the sense that his heart continued to beat and he continued to breathe, his consciousness had been obliterated. In this condition Mr Bland required feeding via a naso-gastric tube, and a urinary catheter. He suffered several infections both of the chest and the urinary system.

It was the unanimous conclusion of all the doctors who examined Mr Bland that he was suffering from a persistent vegetative state from which there was absolutely no hope of recovery. It was the view of the treating consultant that if the feeding tube were to be removed he would die of starvation in 1–2 weeks. As Mr Bland had been in his persistent vegetative state for approximately 3.5 years, the Health Authority with responsibility for his care made an application to the court seeking a declaration that the treating consultants could lawfully discontinue all artificial support including feeding and hydration. The Health Authority's application was supported by Mr Bland's parents. The declarations sought were granted at first instance and at the Court of Appeal. The official solicitor, who acted on behalf of Mr Bland, appealed to the House of Lords.

HELD

Where a patient is incapable of deciding whether or not to consent to treatment, a doctor is under no absolute obligation to prolong life indefinitely. The doctor must act in the best interests of his patient. If it is not in the best interests of the patient to continue to provide life supporting treatment then a doctor is at liberty to withdraw such treatment. This is so even if the effect of the withdrawal of the treatment is that the patient will die. For these purposes, artificial feeding and hydration were undoubtedly medical treatments.

The court were at pains to point out that there was a clear distinction between allowing to die a patient who was already very ill and who was being kept artificially alive, and euthanasia which is taking positive steps to bring about a patient's death. Euthanasia remains unlawful.

Barnett -v- Chelsea & Kensington Hospital Management Committee

[1969] 1 QB 428, [1968] 1 All ER 1068
Keywords: duty of care, duty to treat, causation

FACTS

Three night watchmen had been drinking tea at 05:00 on 1 January 1966. They presented themselves at the Casualty Department of St Stephen's Hospital at around 08:00. They had been vomiting continuously since drinking the tea. On arrival at the hospital they were met by a nurse. One of their number explained their symptoms. Mr Barnett, however, simply laid down. It was clear that he was unwell. The nurse consulted with the casualty officer, explaining the men's symptoms. The doctor instructed the nurse to tell the men to go home, go to bed and contact their own doctors. The nurse complied with this instruction and the men left. Mr Barnett died later on that day. It was concluded that the cause of death was due to arsenical poisoning.

HELD

The following conclusions were reached by the court:

1. The management of the hospital which provides an accident and emergency facility owe a duty of care to persons who present themselves at the department with illness or injury. The duty owed is to exercise the skill and care expected of reasonable doctors and nurses.
2. The casualty officer was negligent in failing to examine Mr Barnett and his colleagues.
3. As there was, unfortunately, no reasonable prospect of Mr Barnett recovering even if his care had been exemplary, the failure of the casualty officer did not cause his death. The claim, therefore failed on causation.

Bolam -v- Friern Hospital Management Committee

[1957] 2 All ER 118, [1957] 1 WLR 582

FACTS

The claimant, John Bolam, was suffering from depression. He was readmitted to Friern Hospital and in August 1954 was treated with electroconvulsive therapy (ECT). In the absence of muscle relaxant drugs, ECT can precipitate convulsive movements involving violent muscular contractions and spasms. Bone fracture is an accepted, if rare, side-effect. The claimant was not warned of the risks of the treatment. It was the practice of the hospital of the time that no relaxant drug should be administered or that the patient should be restrained during the procedure. The treatment was given to the patient while he was lying on the couch. Nurses were positioned on either side of the couch to prevent him from falling off. Unfortunately, during the treatment, the patient suffered bilateral fractures of the acetabula. The claimant alleged that the defendants were negligent in that they failed to administer a muscle relaxant drug prior to treatment, did not provide adequate restraint or control of his movements and failed to adequately warn him of the potential consequences prior to treatment.

It was agreed by the experts for both parties that there was a responsible body of medical opinion who would not have administered muscle relaxant drugs prior to commencing ECT treatment. It was further agreed that there was also a body of opinion which held excessive restraint of a patient led to a greater risk of physical injury during treatment. The claimant's expert did, however, advance the view that patients should be warned of the attendant risks prior to treatment. The defendants expert, however, suggested that a patient should only be warned of the risks if they ask about them.

In directing the jury, McNair J. stated that:

> *A doctor is not negligent if he has acted in accordance with a practice and accepted as proper by a responsible body of medical men skilled in that particular art ...*
>
> *I myself would prefer to put it this way: a doctor is not negligent, if he is acting in accordance with such a practice, merely because there is a body of opinion that takes a contrary view ...*
>
> *Where you get a situation which involves the use of some special skill or competence, then the test whether there has been negligence or not is not the test of the man on top of a Clapham Omnibus, because he has not got the special skill. The test is the standard of the ordinary skilled man exercising and professing to have that special skill. A man need not possess the highest expert skill; it is a well established law that it is sufficient if he exercises the ordinary skill of an ordinary competent man exercising that particular art.*

HELD

The jury found that the treatment of Mr Bolam was not negligent.

Bolitho -v- City & Hackney Health Authority

House of Lords [1998] Lloyds Rep Med 26
Keywords: negligence, causation, application of Bolam to an omission.

FACTS

Patrick Bolitho was a 2-year-old boy who suffered from a patent ductus arteriosus. This was surgically corrected in December 1983. In January 1984 he suffered from croup. He experienced difficulties in breathing and was admitted to hospital. He was discharged home a few days later. The day after his discharge he was readmitted due to his further breathing difficulties.

A paediatric ward sister was concerned about Patrick's condition and contacted the senior paediatric registrar, (SR) to ask the doctor to attend immediately to examine Patrick. The doctor did not arrive and Patrick appeared to recover. Approximately 1.5 hours later a nurse summoned the sister who again could see that Patrick was in some difficulties. The sister therefore again telephoned the SR who was in an out-patient clinic. The SR said that she had asked the senior houseman to attend Patrick. The house officer did not attend because her pager was not working. A short while later Patrick again appeared to have some difficulties with his breathing. While the doctors were being summoned, Patrick collapsed with a cardiac arrest due to his inability to breath. This, in turn, led to severe brain damage.

It was agreed by the parties that it was negligent for the SR or one of her colleagues not to attend in the circumstances described by the ward sister. It was argued on behalf of the claimant that under the circumstances, Patrick should have been intubated. The defendant's experts rejected that argument on the grounds that, in a child of Patrick's age, intubation would have required a general anaesthetic which was not necessary or desirable at that time. The defendants did, however, concede that if Patrick had been intubated prior to his collapse it is likely that the cardiac arrest would not have occurred.

HELD

At first instance, the trial judge found for the defendant. This was on the basis that the claimant had not proved that any competent doctor, given the circumstances, would have intubated Patrick before his collapse.

The claimant appealed because:

1. The judge should not have found the defendants expert to be a reliable witness and to represent a responsible body of medical opinion.
2. Causation was a matter for the judge to decide by applying the normal principles,

i.e. had the admitted negligence caused or materially contributed to Patrick's injury? The judge appeared to be applying the Bolam test to causation.

3. The defendant's expert agreed that under the prevailing circumstances a medical assessment of Patrick should have taken place. As that did not take place, it must have contributed materially to Patrick's injury.

A majority of the Court of Appeal dismissed the claimants appeal because:

1. It was necessary for the judge to decide what course of events would have followed had the SR attended Patrick.
2. In dealing with this hypothetical situation the judge had to rely on the expert evidence available to him.
3. With regard to the SR failure to attend: to make any difference the claimant would have to show that the SR would have intubated had she attended Patrick and that it would be contrary to accepted medical practice not to have so intubated.

The claimant again appealed to the House of Lords. The House of Lords dismissed the appeal because:

1. Even when negligence was admitted, the burden of proving causation still rested on the claimant.
2. The judge had to apply a two-stage test:

   • What would the doctor have done if she had attended Patrick and, if she had not intubated, would such a failure be negligent. If the judge accepted the doctor's evidence that she would not have intubated and the decision not to intubate at that stage was supported by a responsible body of medical opinion, the claimant must fail.
   • As to the question of whether or not the court should accept the defendant's expert as a responsible body of opinion, the court had to be satisfied that those experts putting forward a body of opinion did so on a logical basis. If, however, the judge was not so satisfied, he did not have to accept the expert evidence as being that of a responsible body of practitioners.

Bull & Wakeham -v- Devon Health Authority

[1993] 4 Med LR 117
Keywords: childbirth, twins, medical resources.

FACTS

The first claimant, Mrs Bull, was admitted to the maternity unit of Exeter City Hospital on 21 March 1970. The Health Authority's maternity services were shared between two sites, the obstetric unit being at the Exeter City Hospital, while gynaecological matters were dealt with by the Royal Devon & Exeter Hospital, approximately one mile away. Upon admission it was noted that Mrs Bull was in premature labour of uniovular twins. She was 33 weeks pregnant. The first twin was 'a vertex in brim' and the other was a breach presentation. She was seen by the Senior House Officer, who was inexperienced, and by a registrar with some 5 years experience. The first twin was born at about 19.30. The Senior House Officer asked for the Registrar to be called urgently. Brisk vaginal bleeding ensued which was, clearly, an urgent situation. When the Registrar had not arrived after approximately 25 minutes, the Consultant was summoned. The Consultant came as swiftly as possible but an hour had then elapsed since the birth of the first twin. The Consultant successfully, and speedily, delivered the second twin who is the second claimant in this case. At birth, he was hypoxic and pale. It became clear that he was suffering from profound mental disability and spastic quadriplegia.

His mother commenced court action 9 years later. Her own claim was struck out for being out of time. The claim on behalf of the second twin, however, proceed to trial. The trial judge found in favour of the claimant. The hospital appealed.

HELD

The Court of Appeal confirmed judgement for the second claimant. The issues considered by the court were many and complex. However, the important finding for these purposes is that the Health Authority had been negligent and caused the claimant's brain damage in part because the system of providing experienced cover for obstetric emergencies gave rise to an excessive delay in experienced help arriving at the scene. In the absence of an acceptable explanation for the delay, the standard of care fell below that which the patients were entitled to receive.

Re C (Refusal of medical treatment)

[1994] 1 FLR 31

FACTS

C was a 68-year-old man who was suffering from chronic paranoid schizophrenia. He was a compulsory patient at Broadmoor. In September 1993 he was diagnosed as having gangrene in his right foot and was transferred to an NHS hospital for treatment. He was advised that there should be a below-knee amputation. He was informed that his chances of survival with conservative treatment would be no better than 15%. C refused to consent to the amputation, stating that he would prefer to die than to lose his leg. In the event, the conservative treatment was successful and C survived. C's solicitor asked the hospital to give an undertaking that they would not amputate in any future circumstances where the gangrene recurred. The hospital refused and so C sought an injunction to restrain the hospital from amputating his leg, now or in the future, without his express consent.

HELD

The court acceded to C's request for an injunction. The court held that although C's general capacity was impaired by the schizophrenia, it had not been established that he did not sufficiently understand the nature, purpose and effects of the treatment. The decision-making process could be analysed into three stages: the first, comprehending and retaining the treatment information; the second, believing it; and the third, weighing in the balance to arrive at a choice. The court found that C was able to carry out that exercise and had arrived at the clear choice.

Emeh -v- Kensington & Chelsea & Westminster Area Health Authority

[1985] 2 WLR 233 (CA)
Keywords: failed sterilisation, wrongful birth, novus actus interveniens, damages.

FACTS

The claimant, Kathleen Emeh, was a married woman who had three healthy children. In May 1976 she underwent an abortion and sterilisation operation at St Stephens Hospital, London. She discovered in January 1997 that she was approximately 20 weeks pregnant. She decided against having a further abortion. She was delivered of a child (Elizabeth) who was found to be congenitally abnormal. She sued for damages in respect of the failed sterilisation. The defendants argued that Mrs Emeh was the cause of her own misfortune in as much as she refused to have an abortion.

HELD

The court concluded that, except in the most unusual circumstances, the court could not declare it unreasonable for a woman to decline to have an abortion where there was no evidence that any medical or psychiatric grounds existed for terminating that particular pregnancy. The claimant's refusal to have an abortion did not, therefore, supplant the surgeon's negligence as the cause of the birth of a child whether healthy or abnormal.
[N.B. please now see *McFarlane -v- Tayside Health Authority.*]

Gillick -v- West Norfolk & Wisbech Area Health Authority

House of Lords [1986] AC112, [1985] 3 All ER 402
Keywords: consent, minors parental objections.

FACTS

The case was brought by Mrs Victoria Gillick who was the mother of five daughters under the age of 16. It related to a Department of Health and Social Security circular which contained advice to doctors. The circular suggested that a doctor consulted by a girl under the age of 16 who sought family planning would not be acting unlawfully if he prescribed contraceptives for the girl so long as he was acting in her best interests. The circular also proposed that it was permissible for a doctor to prescribe contraception without the consent of the girl's parents under appropriate circumstances.

The claimant, Mrs Gillick, brought the action seeking a declaration against the DHSS and the Area Health Authority to the effect that the circular was unlawful, and a further declaration against the Area Health Authority providing that no doctor employed by the authority would give contraceptive advice or treatment to any of her children under the age of 16 without her consent.

The Court of Appeal granted the declarations as sought. The matter was then appealed to the House of Lords.

HELD

The House of Lords found that the declarations had been granted inappropriately. Their Lordships held that a girl under 16 did not lack legal capacity to consent to contraceptive advice and treatment by a doctor merely by reason of her age. The doctor had discretion to give advice or treatment to the child without her parents' consent, provided that the girl was old enough to have sufficient understanding to know what was being proposed. The question was not simply a matter of parental consent being required up to a specific age. Their Lordships made it clear that a child, under the age of 15, who had sufficient understanding, was more than capable of consenting to a wide range of treatments, notwithstanding parental objections.

Hotson -v- East Berkshire Area Health Authority

House of Lords [1987] AC 750, [1987] 2 All ER 909
Keywords: loss of chance, causation, substandard treatment.

FACTS

The claimant, Stephen Hotson, was at the material time, 13 years of age. On 26 April 1977 he climbed a tree, lost his hold and fell some 12 feet to the ground. He was taken to St Luke's Hospital, Maidenhead. He was examined by the hospital staff who failed to diagnose an acute traumatic fracture of the left femoral epiphysis. He was discharged home. On 1 May 1977 he returned to hospital. X-rays of his hip disclosed the correct diagnosis. He had suffered an avascular necrosis of the epiphysis. This caused a disability of the hip joint with the added complication that osteoarthritis was now virtually certain. He sued the Health Authority who admitted negligence in failing to diagnose the injury upon his first presentation.

The trial judge found that even if the Health Authority had correctly diagnosed and treated the claimant upon first presentation there was a high probability (75%) that his injury would have followed the same course in any event. The breach of duty in failing to diagnose the injury made the 75% risk a certainty. The trial judge therefore awarded the claimant 25% of the damages, which he would have received upon full recovery. The Court of Appeal upheld the judge's decision.

HELD

The House of Lords, however, took a different view. In civil claims, the claimant has to prove his case on the balance of probabilities. If something is more probable than not, it is taken as being proved. In this particular case, the judge's finding of fact that, even had the correct diagnosis been made at first presentation, there was a 75% chance the injury would have followed the same course in any event meant that this was considered to be a certainty. The correct analysis was, therefore, that the claimant should fail. It was not appropriate to apportion damages based on a 'loss of chance'.

McFarlane -v- Tayside Health Board

House of Lords [2000] Lloyds Rep Med 1
Keywords: damages, failed vasectomy, healthy child born, recoverability of costs of upbringing.

FACTS

Mr McFarlane underwent a vasectomy. He was later told that his sperm counts were negative so he and his wife could dispense with further contraceptive measures. The couple, who already had four healthy children, acted upon this advice. Mrs McFarlane became pregnant and their fifth child was born. The child was perfectly healthy.

Mr and Mrs McFarlane commenced proceedings against the Tayside Health Board, claiming damages for Mrs McFarlane's pain and suffering in going through the pregnancy and birth and the costs of maintenance of the child. Mr and Mrs McFarlane, in bringing the claim, confirmed that they loved and cared for the child as with the rest of the family.

This was a claim which initially proceeded through the Scottish court system. It was dismissed at first instance and restored on appeal. The Health Board appealed to the House of Lords.

HELD

The claim could be broadly divided into two sections. A claim by Mr and Mrs McFarlane for the costs of bringing up their child and, second, a claim by Mrs McFarlane in respect of the pain and suffering resulting from the pregnancy and birth. Their Lordships allowed the appeal of the Health Board against the costs of bringing up the child but dismissed the appeal in respect of the pain and suffering of Mrs McFarlane.

The case has, therefore, reversed a line of authorities which formally permitted the recovery of the cost of bringing up a healthy child born as a result of failed vasectomy. This is clearly a policy decision. The principal reason given by their Lordships appears to be that, while the costs of bringing up a child can be calculated, benefit of having a child is immeasurable in financial terms. Parents cannot have the benefit of a child without also accepting the responsibilities which go with those benefits. It is not right, therefore, that the defendants should suffer the financial consequences of bringing up the child while the parents reap the benefits.

McKay & Another -v- Essex Area Health Authority & Another

Court of Appeal [1982] 1 QB 1166
Keywords: wrongful birth, failure to diagnose.

FACTS

The claimant, Mary McKay, was born in August 1975 with severe congenital disabilities. It was alleged that, prior to her birth, her mother became infected with rubella. Her mother consulted her doctor who took blood samples, which were sent to a hospital laboratory. It was further alleged that the mother was informed that she and her unborn child had not been infected with rubella during the pregnancy and, therefore, that she need not consider an abortion. The claimant sued the doctor and hospital authorities. Her claim fell into two parts: the first was that she was injured by reason of the doctor's failure to inject immuno globulins into her mother; the second was for the failure to counsel her mother as to the possibilities of the termination of the pregnancy.

HELD

The second arm of her claim was an action for 'wrongful life'. There was no duty owed by a doctor to an unborn child to bring about the death of that child.

[N.B. the effect of the Congenital Disabilities (Civil Liability) Act 1976 is that no child born after its passing can have a right of action for 'wrongful life'.]

McLoughlin -v- O'Brian

House of Lords [1982] 2 All ER 298
Keywords: personal injury, nervous shock, duty of care to plaintiff not at accident, foreseeability of harm.

FACTS

Mr and Mrs McLoughlin had four children. On the day of the incident in question their eldest son, who was 17, was driving his father, Thomas McLoughlin, and his two young sisters, Kathleen (7) and Gillian (3), along the A604 from Cambridge to Haverhill. The vehicle was involved in a collision with a lorry which had, itself, previously collided with another lorry. There is no argument that the accident was caused by the negligence of the driver of the first lorry. Following the accident, Mr McLoughlin and his three children were taken to the local hospital. Mr McLoughlin and the two older children suffered various fractures and concussion. Gillian, aged 3, was killed.

At the time of the incident, Mrs McLoughlin was at home. A neighbour called to the house and explained that there had been an accident in which her family had been involved. The neighbour then took Mrs McLoughlin to the hospital where she was told that Gillian had died. She then passed through a corridor in the hospital where she saw each family member in turn and witnessed their pain and suffering. As a result of these traumatic events she suffered nervous shock which went beyond the normal grief reaction which any person could be expected to suffer under the circumstances. Mrs McLoughlin sought to recover from the defendants damages for her severe and permanent nervous condition.

At first instance the judge dismissed the claims on the grounds that her injury was not reasonably foreseeable. Mrs McLoughlin appealed to the Court of Appeal. This appeal was unsuccessful and the claimant therefore appealed to the House of Lords.

HELD

Their Lordships granted the appeal. It was held that the test of liability for damages arising from nervous shock was reasonable foreseeability of the claimant being injured by nervous shock as a result of the defendants' negligence. The claimant was, therefore, entitled to recover damages because, even though she was not at or near the scene of the accident at the time or shortly afterwards, the nervous shock suffered by her was reasonably foreseeable.

Roe -v- Minister of Health & Another

Court of Appeal [1954] 2 QB 66
Keywords: anaesthetics, res ipsa loquitur.

FACTS

In October 1947 the claimant, Cecil Roe, was operated on at the Chesterfield & North Derbyshire Royal Hospital. The anaesthetist was appointed as the visiting anaesthetist at the hospital. The glass ampules containing the anaesthetic had been immersed in phenol. It was alleged that the phenol had percolated through invisible cracks in each ampule thereby contaminating the spinal anaesthetic. The anaesthetic was administered to the claimant. The risk of this happening was first drawn to the attention of the anaesthetist by a book published in 1951. Mr Roe, and another patient on the same list, suffered paralysis from the waist down as a result of spinal damage caused by the anaesthetic. The trial judge found for the defendants. The claimants appealed.

HELD

The Court of Appeal found that the hospital authority was liable for the acts of the anaesthetist. He formed part of their staff, even though he was a visiting member. The maxim of res ipsa loquitur applied. The defendants had, however, explained how the accident had occurred. The trial took place after the publication of the explanation in 1951 but the incident took place in 1947. It was not, therefore, appropriate to impute into the anaesthetist's knowledge, which was not available at the relevant time. Lord Denning stated, inter alia,

> We must not look at the 1947 accident with 1954 spectacles. The Judge acquitted Dr Graham of negligence and we should uphold his decision.

Sidaway -v- Board of Governors of the Bethlem Royal Hospital & The Maudsley Hospital

House of Lords, [1985] AC 871, [1985] 1 All ER 643
Keywords: surgery, risk of operation, informed consent, disclosure of risks.

FACTS

In October 1974, the claimant, Mrs Amy Sidaway, was admitted to the Maudsley Hospital. She had persistent pain in her right arm and shoulder and left forearm. A myelogram was performed. A surgeon decided to operate. The procedure consisted of a laminectomy of the fourth cervical vertebrae and a facetectomy or foraminectomy of the disc spaces between the fourth and fifth cervical vertebrae. The fourth cervical nerve root was freed by the removal of the facets from the fourth vertebrae. An attempt was made to free the nerve within the foramin. During the procedure Mrs Sidaway's spinal cord was damaged, resulting in severe paralysis. It was accepted that the operation had not been negligently performed. Mrs Sidaway's claim was based on the failure to warn her of the risk of damage to her spinal cord. There were two particular risks of which Mrs Sidaway claimed she should have been warned. The first was the damage to her spinal cord. The risk of this occurring was put at less than 1%. There was also a combined risk of damage to the nerve root and/or spinal cord, which was put at 2%. It was found that the surgeon had mentioned the possibility of disturbing the nerve root but had not mentioned the risk to the spinal cord. It was also found that there was a responsible body of competent neurosurgeons who did not frighten the patient by talking about death or paralysis. The trial judge dismissed the claim.

HELD

Their Lordships concluded that, as there was a responsible body of medical opinion which would have given a similar warning as that givin by the surgeon, the claim failed. Their Lordships went onto point out that the Bolam test applied equally to the advice given to a patient as it did to other aspects of their care.

Wilshire -v- Essex Health Authority

House of Lords [1988] 1 All ER 871, [1988] 2 WLR
Keywords: causation, burden of proof, standard of treatment.

The claimant, Martin Wilsher, was born on 15 December 1978 at the Princess Alexandra Hospital, Harlow. He was nearly 3 months premature. He was a tiny baby who required support for his breathing. To monitor the level of oxygen in the arterial blood of such infants, it was standard practice to pass a catheter into the aorta via the umbilical artery. A Senior House Officer (SHO) carried out this procedure early on 16 December 1978. The SHO arranged for an X-ray and called the Registrar to inspect what had been done. Neither doctor realised that the X-ray disclosed that the catheter was in fact sited in a vein and not the aorta. The results of the monitor, therefore, revealed the level of oxygen in venous blood not arterial blood. The readings were, as a result, much lower than would have been obtained had an arterial blood sample been monitored. Increased levels of oxygen were administered in an effort to raise the oxygen level in what the doctors' thought was the arterial blood. Early in the morning of 17 December 1978, the SHO realised that the catheter was in the wrong place. It was duly repositioned. It was clear that the oxygen levels had been excessively high for 8–12 hours. The claimant required oxygen for approximately another 11 weeks. During this time he suffered high oxygen levels in his arterial blood on five subsequent occasions. The claimant was subsequently found to suffer from retrolental fibroplasia (RLF) and was almost blind. A claim was pursued against the Health Authority on the basis that the excess of oxygen in his early weeks caused the RLF. At first instance, the trial judge found in his favour. The Court of Appeal affirmed the judge's decision insofar as it related to the negligence affecting the period 16–17 December, though not any subsequent period. The court further held that the SHO was not negligent in as much as he inserted the catheter into a vein rather than an artery. The Registrar had, however, been negligent in that he failed to appreciate the catheter was situated in the wrong place. The SHO was, however, entitled to rely on the checking of his work by his supervisor.

The Health Authority appealed. The question of negligence was not disputed. The question before the House of Lords was that of causation.

HELD

Their Lordships included that the onus of proving causation rested with the plaintiff. He had to establish that the raised oxygen levels in his arterial blood on the 16 and 17

December probably caused or materially contributed to his RLF. The fact that excess oxygen was one of a number of different factors that could have caused the RLF was not in any way determinative of the question as to whether, in fact, the excess oxygen did cause or materially contribute to the injury. There was a considerable divergence of expert opinion as to whether or not the excess oxygen did cause or materially contribute to the plaintiff's RLF.

Appendix 3
Pre-action protocol for the resolution of clinical disputes[1]

(With kind permission from Civil Court Service 2001, published by Jordan Publishing Limited, Bristol)

General note

The protocol has been widely disseminated across all areas of clinical practice including NHS Trusts and private providers. Hence, all health care providers should have full knowledge of its scope and operation.

Executive summary

1. The Clinical Disputes Forum is a multi-disciplinary body which was formed in 1997, as a result of Lord Woolf's 'Access to Justice' inquiry. One of the aims of the Forum is to find less adversarial and more cost-effective ways of resolving disputes about health care and medical treatment. The names and addresses of the Chairman and Secretary of the Forum can be found at Annex E.
2. This protocol is the Forum's first major initiative. It has been drawn up carefully, including extensive consultations with most of the key stakeholders in the medico-legal system.
3. The protocol:

   - encourages a climate of openness when something has 'gone wrong' with a patient's treatment or the patient is dissatisfied with that treatment and/or the outcome. This reflects the new and developing requirements for clinical governance within health care
   - provides **general guidance** on how this more open culture might be achieved when disputes arise
   - recommends a **timed sequence** of steps for patients and health care providers, and their advisers, to follow when a dispute arises. This should facilitate and speed up exchanging relevant information and increase the prospects that disputes can be resolved without resort to legal action.

4. This protocol has been prepared by a working party of the Clinical Disputes Forum. It has the support of the Lord Chancellor's Department, the Department of Health and NHS Executive, the Law Society, the Legal Aid Board and many other key organisations.

1 Why this protocol?

MISTRUST IN HEALTH CARE DISPUTES

1.1 The number of complaints and claims against hospitals, GPs, dentists and private health care providers is growing as patients become more prepared to question the treatment they are given, to seek explanations of what happened, and to seek appropriate redress. Patients may require further treatment, an apology, assurances about future action or compensation. These trends are unlikely to change. The Patients' Charter encourages patients to have high expectations, and a revised NHS Complaints Procedure was implemented in 1996. The civil justice reforms and new Rules of Court should make litigation quicker, more user friendly and less expensive.

1.2 It is clearly in the interests of patients, health care professionals and providers that patients' concerns, complaints and claims arising from their treatment are resolved as quickly, efficiently and professionally as possible. A climate of mistrust and lack of openness can seriously damage the patient/clinician relationship, unnecessarily prolong disputes (especially litigation), and reduce the resources available for treating patients. It may also cause additional work for, and lower the morale of, health care professionals.

1.3 At present there is often mistrust by both sides. This can mean that patients fail to raise their concerns with the health care provider as early as possible. Sometimes patients may pursue a complaint or claim which has little merit, due to a lack of sufficient information and understanding. It can also mean that patients become reluctant, once advice has been taken on a potential claim, to disclose sufficient information to enable the provider to investigate that claim efficiently and, where appropriate, resolve it.

1.4 On the side of the health care provider, this mistrust can be shown in a reluctance to be honest with patients, a failure to provide prompt clear explanations, especially of adverse outcomes (whether or not there may have been negligence) and a tendency to 'close ranks' once a claim is made.

WHAT NEEDS TO CHANGE

1.5 If that mistrust is to be removed, and a more co-operative culture is to develop:

- health care professionals and providers need to adopt a constructive approach to complaints and claims. They should accept that concerned patients are entitled to an explanation and an apology, if warranted, and to appropriate redress in the event of negligence. An overly defensive approach is not in the long-term interest of their main goal: patient care
- patients should recognise that unintended and/or unfortunate consequences of medical treatment can only be rectified if they are brought to the attention of the health care provider as soon as possible.

1.6 A protocol which sets out 'ground rules' for the handling of disputes at their early stages should, if it is to be subscribed to, and followed:

- encourage greater openness between the parties
- encourage parties to find the most appropriate way of resolving the particular dispute
- reduce delay and costs
- reduce the need for litigation.

WHY THIS PROTOCOL NOW?

1.7 Lord Woolf in his 'Access to Justice' Report in July 1996, concluded that major causes of costs and delay in medical negligence litigation occur at the pre-action stage. He recommended that patients and their advisers, and health care providers, should work more closely together to try to resolve disputes co-operatively, rather than proceed to litigation. He specifically recommended a pre-action protocol for medical negligence cases.

1.8 A fuller summary of Lord Woolf's recommendations is at Annex D.

WHERE THE PROTOCOL FITS IN

1.9 Protocols serve the needs of litigation and pre-litigation practice, especially:

- predictability in the time needed for steps pre-proceedings
- standardisation of relevant information, including records and documents to be disclosed.

1.10 Building upon Lord Woolf's recommendations, the Lord Chancellor's Department is now promoting the adoption of protocols in specific areas, including medical negligence.

1.11 It is recognised that contexts differ significantly. For example, patients tend to have an ongoing relationship with a GP, more so than with a hospital; clinical staff in the NHS are often employees, while those in the private sector may be contractors; providing records quickly may be relatively easy for GPs and dentists, but can be a complicated procedure in a large multi-department hospital. The protocol which follows is intended to be sufficiently broadly based, and flexible, to apply to all aspects of the health service: primary and secondary; public and private sectors.

ENFORCEMENT OF THE PROTOCOL AND SANCTIONS

1.12 The civil justice reforms will be implemented in April 1999. One new set of court rules and procedures is replacing the existing rules for both the High Court and county courts. This and the personal injury protocol are being published with the Rules, Practice Directions and key court forms. The courts will be able to treat the standards set in protocols as the normal reasonable approach to pre-action conduct.

1.13 If proceedings are issued it will be for the court to decide whether non-compliance with a protocol should merit sanctions. Guidance on the court's likely approach will be given from time to time in practice directions.

1.14 If the court has to consider the question of compliance after proceedings have begun it will not be concerned with minor infringements, e.g. failure by a short period to provide relevant information. One minor breach will not entitle the 'innocent' party to abandon following the protocol. The court will look at the effect of non-compliance on the other party when deciding whether to impose sanctions.

2 The aims of the protocol

2.1 The *general* aims of the protocol are:

- to maintain/restore the patient/health care provider relationship
- to resolve as many disputes as possible without litigation.

2.2 The *specific* objectives are:

OPENNESS

- To encourage early communication of the perceived problem between patients and health care providers.
- To encourage patients to voice any concerns or dissatisfaction with their treatment as soon as practicable.
- To encourage health care providers to develop systems of early reporting and investigation for serious adverse treatment outcomes and to provide full and prompt explanations to dissatisfied patients.
- To ensure that sufficient information is disclosed by both parties to enable each to understand the other's perspective and case, and to encourage early resolution.

TIMELINESS

- To provide an early opportunity for health care providers to identify cases where an investigation is required and to carry out that investigation promptly.
- To encourage primary and private health care providers to involve their defence organisations or insurers at an early stage.
- To ensure that all relevant medical records are provided to patients or their appointed representatives on request, to a realistic timetable by any health care provider.
- To ensure that relevant records not in health care providers' possession are made available to them by patients and their advisers at an appropriate stage;
- Where a resolution is not achievable to lay the ground to enable litigation to proceed on a reasonable timetable, at a reasonable and proportionate cost and to limit the matters in contention.

- To discourage the prolonged pursuit of unmeritorious claims and the prolonged defence of meritorious claims.

AWARENESS OF OPTIONS

- To ensure that patients and health care providers are made aware of the available options to pursue and resolve disputes and what each might involve.

2.3 This protocol does not attempt to be prescriptive about a number of related clinical governance issues which will have a bearing on health care providers' ability to meet the standards within the protocol. Good clinical governance requires the following to be considered:

- **Clinical risk management:** the protocol does not provide any detailed guidance to health care providers on clinical risk management or the adoption of risk management systems and procedures. This must be a matter for the NHS Executive, the National Health Service Litigation Authority, individual Trusts and providers, including GPs, dentists and the private sector. However, effective co-ordinated, focussed clinical risk management strategies and procedures can help in managing risk and in the early identification and investigation of adverse outcomes.
- **Adverse outcome reporting:** the protocol does not provide any detailed guidance on which adverse outcomes should trigger an investigation. However, health care providers should have in place procedures for such investigations, including recording of statements of key witnesses. These procedures should also cover when and how to inform patients that an adverse outcome has occurred.
- **The professional's duty to report**: the protocol does not recommend changes to the codes of conduct of professionals in health care, or attempt to impose a specific duty on those professionals to report known adverse outcomes or untoward incidents. Lord Woolf in his final report suggested that the professional bodies might consider this. The General Medical Council is preparing guidance to doctors about their duty to report adverse incidents and to co-operate with inquiries.

3 The protocol

3.1 This protocol is not a comprehensive code governing all the steps in clinical disputes. Rather it attempts to set out a **code of good practice** which parties should follow when litigation might be a possibility.

3.2 The **commitments** section of the protocol summarises the guiding principles which health care providers and patients and their advisers are invited to endorse when dealing with patient dissatisfaction with treatment and its outcome, and with potential complaints and claims.

3.3 The **steps** section sets out in a more prescriptive form, a recommended sequence of actions to be followed if litigation is a prospect.

GOOD PRACTICE COMMITMENTS

3.4 **Health care providers should:**

- Ensure that **key staff,** including claims and litigation managers, are appropriately trained and have some knowledge of health care law, and of complaints procedures and civil litigation practice and procedure;
- Develop an approach to clinical **governance** that ensures that clinical practice is delivered to commonly accepted standards and that this is routinely monitored through a system of clinical audit and clinical risk management (particularly adverse outcome investigation).
- Set up **adverse outcome reporting systems** in all specialties to record and investigate unexpected serious adverse outcomes as soon as possible. Such systems can enable evidence to be gathered quickly, which makes it easier to provide an accurate explanation of what happened and to defend or settle any subsequent claims.
- Use the results of adverse **incidents and complaints positively** as a guide to how to improve services to patients in the future.
- Ensure that **patients receive clear and comprehensible information** in an accessible form about how to raise their concerns or complaints.
- Establish **efficient and effective systems of recording and storing patient records,** notes, diagnostic reports and X-rays, and to retain these in accordance with Department of Health guidance (currently for a minimum of 8 years in the case of adults, and all obstetric and paediatric notes for children until they reach the age of 25).
- **Advise patients** of a serious adverse outcome and provide on request to the patient or the patient's representative an oral or written explanation of what happened, information on further steps open to the patient, including where appropriate an offer of future treatment to rectify the problem, an apology, changes in procedure which will benefit patients and/or compensation.

3.5 **Patients and their advisers should:**

- **Report any concerns and dissatisfaction** to the health care provider as soon as is reasonable to enable that provider to offer clinical advice where possible, to advise the patient if anything has gone wrong and take appropriate action.
- Consider the **full range of options** available following an adverse outcome with which a patient is dissatisfied, including a request for an explanation, a meeting, a complaint and other appropriate dispute resolution methods (including mediation) and negotiation, not only litigation.
- **Inform the health care provider when the patient is satisfied** that the matter has been concluded: legal advisers should notify the provider when they are no longer acting for the patient, particularly if proceedings have not started.

PROTOCOL STEPS

3.6 The steps of this protocol which follow have been kept deliberately simple. An illustration of the likely sequence of events in a number of health care situations is at Annex A.

OBTAINING THE HEALTH RECORDS

3.7 Any request for records by the **patient or their adviser** should:

- **provide sufficient information** to alert the health care provider where an adverse outcome has been serious or had serious consequences
- be as **specific as possible** about the records which are required.

3.8 Requests for copies of the patient's clinical records should be made using the Law Society and Department of Health approved **standard forms** (enclosed at Annex B), adapted as necessary.

3.9 The copy records should be provided **within 40 days** of the request and for a cost not exceeding the charges permissible under the Access to Health Records Act 1990.

3.10 In the rare circumstances that the health care provider is in difficulty in complying with the request within 40 days, the **problem should be explained** quickly and details given of what is being done to resolve it.

3.11 It will not be practicable for health care providers to investigate in detail each case when records are requested. But health care providers should **adopt a policy on which cases will be investigated** (see paragraph 3.5 on clinical governance and adverse outcome reporting).

3.12 If the health care provider fails to provide the health records within 40 days, the patient or their adviser can then apply to the court for an **order for pre-action disclosure**. The new Civil Procedure Rules should make pre-action applications to the court easier. The court will also have the power to impose costs sanctions for unreasonable delay in providing records.

3.13 If either the patient or the health care provider considers **additional health records are required from a third party,** in the first instance these should be requested by or through the patient. Third party health care providers are expected to co-operate. The Civil Procedure Rules will enable patients and health care providers to apply to the court for pre-action disclosure by third parties.

General note: The disclosure of records envisaged by the protocol is not intended to be restricted to those records discloseable under Access to Health Records Act 1990, Data Protection Act 1998, Supreme Court Act 1981, ss33, 34 and County Courts Act

1984, ss 52,53. Instead the protocol envisages that both an intended party to proceedings and a non-party should, upon proper request as outlined above, provide copies of all records relevant to the case. 'Records' has a wide interpretation and will include all clinical documents, scans, test results and correspondence.

The intention is that the parties should have available all documentation necessary to enable a detailed investigation of the case.

'Within 40 days' (paras 3.9 and 3.12): This time limit was deemed reasonable to permit a health care provider to assemble and copy the relevant records. In general terms, no application to court under CPR r 31.16 should be made within this time limit. Consistent with the overriding objective, flexibility maybe required; for example, in the context of a case where the limitation period is due to expire imminently, a shortened time scale may be appropriate, or in a case where access to records is difficult because of ongoing treatment, more time may be necessary.

Access to Health Records Act 1990: This legislation has now been repealed except for sections dealing with requests for access to records relating to a deceased person. Requests for access to records of deceased persons will continue to be made under that Act but requests for access to health records relating to living individuals will now fall within the scope of the Data Protection Act 1998. This Act was implemented on 1 March 2000 and governs both manual and automated records.

Data Protection Act 1998: A guidance note on the operation of the Act was issued by the Office of the Data Protection Commissioner in August 2000 and provides helpful information on the applicability of the legislation to the subject of access to health records. It is important to note that the Data Protection Act 1998 defines a 'health record' as being any record which consists of information relating to the physical or mental health or condition of an individual and has been made by or on behalf of a health professional in connection with the care of that individual. The guidance note makes clear that this definition has a wide interpretation and will, for example, include radiographic material.

Cost: This has been a vexed issue in the past with wide discrepancies around the country. The protocol intended that a reasonable limit should be imposed in line with the charging structure thus described in the Access to Health Records Act 1990. The position has been significantly clarified by the Data Protection Act 1998 and is as follows:

- A maximum fee of £10 for granting access to health records which are automatically processed or are recorded with the intention that they be so processed.
- A maximum fee of £50 for granting access to manual records, or a mixture of manual and automated records.
- There is no provision for there to be any separate or additional charge for copying or postage.

- There is no charge for allowing an individual to inspect records, where the request relates to recently created records, i.e. where at least some of the records were made within the period of 40 days prior to the date of request (thus replicating the previous provision of the Access to Health Records Act 1990).
- Note the position regarding records of a deceased person remains governed by the Access to Health Records Act 1990.

This statutory regulation of charging now provides consistency and will eliminate, for example, the variation of charges being requested by general practitioners.

Health records from a third party (para 3.13): Whilst CPR r 31.16 limits disclosure before proceedings start to documents from those respondents likely to be a party to proceedings, the protocol is wider and requires third party disclosure. This may be highly relevant in clinical negligence cases to help determine issues such as causation. Hence, note the requirement for third party co-operation. Two points arise:

- query whether the wide power of CPR r 31.18 may be applied to support the protocol intent and, thus, in the event of non co-operation by a third party, permit a pre-action application to court, or;
- in the alternative, if a post commencement of proceedings application for third party disclosure is made, that third party may bear a costs penalty for failure to co-operate with a protocol request.

LETTER OF CLAIM

3.14 Annex Cl to this protocol provides a **template for the recommended contents of a letter of claim:** the level of detail will need to be varied to suit the particular circumstances.

3.15 If, following the receipt and analysis of the records, and the receipt of any further advice (including from experts if necessary see Section 4), the patient/adviser decides that there are grounds for a claim, they should then send, as soon as practicable, to the health care provider/potential defendant, a **letter of claim.**

3.16 This letter should contain a **clear summary of the facts** on which the claim is based, including the alleged adverse outcome, and the **main allegations of negligence.** It should also describe the **patient's injuries,** and present condition and prognosis. The **financial loss** incurred by the plaintiff should be outlined with an indication of the heads of damage to be claimed and the scale of the loss, unless this is impracticable.

3.17 In more complex cases, a **chronology** of the relevant events should be provided, particularly if the patient has been treated by a number of different health care providers.

3.18 The letter of claim **should refer to any relevant documents,** including health records, and if possible enclose copies of any of those which will not already be in the potential defendant's possession, e.g. any relevant general practitioner records if the plaintiff's claim is against a hospital.

3.19 **Sufficient information** must be given to enable the health care provider defendant to **commence investigations** and to put an initial valuation on the claim.

3.20 Letters of claim are **not** intended to have the same formal status as a **pleading,** nor should any sanctions necessarily apply if the letter of claim and any subsequent statement of claim in the proceedings differ.

3.21 **Proceedings should not be issued until after 3 months from the letter of claim,** unless there is a limitation problem and/or the patient's position needs to be protected by early issue.

3.22 The patient or their adviser may want to make an **offer to settle** the claim at this early stage by putting forward an amount of compensation which would be satisfactory (possibly including any costs incurred to date). If an offer to settle is made, generally this should be supported by a medical report which deals with the injuries, condition and prognosis, and by a schedule of loss and supporting documentation. The level of detail necessary will depend on the value of the claim. Medical reports may not be necessary where there is no significant continuing injury, and a detailed schedule may not be necessary in a low value case. The Civil Procedure Rules are expected to set out the legal and procedural requirements for making offers to settle.

Recommended contents (para 3.19): Note paras 3.14 and 3.16 which should be read in the context of para 3.19. The level of detail to be provided will vary depending upon the complexity of the case. The protocol is not intended to be overly prescriptive; disclosure of a report on condition and prognosis is not mandated; a comprehensive schedule of financial loss is not required (in a smaller case an analysis of the financial losses may be appropriate; in a major injury case, which will require expert analysis of quantum issues, a summary of the main heads of claim may be sufficient). The intention is not to create a welter of case law interpreting whether a letter of claim is protocol-compliant but rather to instill a sensible level of exchange of information consistent with the overall aim of the protocol.

Since the Pre-Action Protocol for the Resolution of Clinical Disputes was produced the Access to Justice Act 1999 has come into force and further extended the role of conditional fee agreements. Consequently, PDProt was amended on 3 July 2000 and paras 4A.1 and 4A.2 were added. These paragraphs imply that notification of a funding arrangement should be given during the protocol. This may mean that it would be appropriate to include details (in the letter of claim if applicable).

THE RESPONSE

3.23 Attached at Annex C2 is a template for the suggested contents of the **letter of response.**

3.24 The health care provider should **acknowledge the letter of claim within 14 days of receipt** and should identify who will be dealing with the matter.

3.25 The health care provider should, **within 3 months of the letter of claim, provide a reasoned answer:**

- If the **claim is admitted** the health care provider should say so in clear terms.
- If only **part of the claim is admitted** the health care provider should make clear which issues of breach of duty and/or causation are admitted and which are denied and why.
- It is intended that any admissions will **be binding**.
- If the claim is denied, this should include specific comments on the allegations of negligence, and if a synopsis or chronology of relevant events has been provided and is disputed, the health care provider's version of those events.
- Where additional documents are relied upon, e.g. an internal protocol, copies should be provided.

3.26 If the patient has made an offer to settle, the health care provider should **respond to that offer** in the response letter, preferably with reasons. The provider may make its own offer to settle at this stage, either as a counter-offer to the patient's, or of its own accord, but should accompany any offer by any supporting medical evidence, and/or by any other evidence in relation to the value of the claim which is in the health care provider's possession.

3.27 If the parties reach agreement on liability, but time is needed to resolve the value of the claim, they should aim to agree a reasonable period.

'Not intended to have . . . formal status' (para 3.20): This is important. The letter of claim is intended to provide adequate information to enable a respondent to understand, in general terms, the nature of the case it has to meet. It is recognised that after the submission of that letter, the claimant's position may vary, for example, because of the impact of the letter of response, receipt of further information or expert advice. Hence, whilst sanctions are not expressly ruled out by para 3.20, it is intended that they should be applied only in the most appropriate of cases.

'Three months' (para 3.21): This period is intended to dovetail with the time for response (see below). It is recognised that, for example, limitation difficulties may require earlier issue. Where this arises, then consistent with both the aim of the protocol and the overriding objective, flexibility will be required so that, for example, it may be appropriate to extend the time for delivery of full particulars of claim until after the response letter has been received; a stay may be sensible to permit the sending of a response letter and to enable the parties to discuss the case.

'Offer to settle' (para 3.22): This provision is intended to dovetail with Pt 36. Note that, in the context of a clinical negligence case, a claimant wishing to make an offer before proceedings have been commenced should generally provide information in support of quantum, e.g. a report on condition and prognosis.

'Letter of response' (para 3.23): The response should reciprocate the intention of the letter of claim and thus provide a detailed answer to the claim sufficient to enable the patient/patient's adviser to understand the position. A bare denial is unacceptable. Hence, note the detail required by para 3.25 and envisaged by the template letter at Annex C2.

'Within 3 months' (para 3.25): Several points arise:

- This time limit starts to run from the date of receipt of the letter of claim. Thus, the 14-day period for acknowledgement of receipt falls within the 3 months.
- Anecdotal evidence suggests some difficulty is being encountered in responding within this period. This will be considered when the protocol is reviewed but note that:
    a. 3 months was felt by all on the CDF to be a reasonable period – it balances the patient's desire for a speedy response against the health care provider's need for time to investigate and consult with those involved.
    b. Consistent with the Good Practice Commitments, a health care provider is expected pro-actively to identify adverse outcomes, report them and tell the patient. Hence, there may well be and possibly should be a level of awareness before even the request for records is received.
    c. The receipt of the request for records should alert as to the possibility of a claim and possibly prompt investigation.
    d. There may well be knowledge of the position because of an internal investigation or pursuit of a formal complaint, e.g. under the NHS complaints system.

'Admissions will be binding' (para 3.25): This is a fundamental point. It is not intended that there should be any facility to resile from an admission. This contrasts with CPR r 14.1(5) (the facility given there is not intended to apply in the protocol situation). An admission made under the protocol will be binding when proceedings are later commenced.

'Respond to that offer' (para 3.26): Note the requirement to respond to an offer to settle in this situation (not something required by Pt 36) and note the obligation, if making a counter offer, to provide documentation in support.

4 Experts

General note: The protocol deliberately does not prescribe any procedures with regard to the use of experts in contradistinction to the Pre-Action Protocol for Personal Injury Claims. It was recognised that clinical negligence litigation involved special or unusual areas of difficulty and that, particularly on issues of breach of duty and causation, each party should be able to access experts of their own choosing. Consistent with this approach, there is no requirement to identify experts to be instructed in advance to the other side and no need to tender names.

4.1 In clinical negligence disputes **expert opinions** may be needed:

- on breach of duty and causation
- on the patient's condition and prognosis
- to assist in valuing aspects of the claim.

4.2 The civil justice reforms and the new **Civil Procedure Rules will encourage** economy in the use of experts and a **less adversarial expert culture.** It is recognised that in clinical negligence disputes, the parties and their advisers will require flexibility in their approach to expert evidence. Decisions on whether experts might be instructed jointly, and on whether reports might be disclosed sequentially or by exchange, should rest with the parties and their advisers. Sharing expert evidence may be appropriate on issues relating to the value of the claim. However, this protocol does not attempt to be prescriptive on issues in relation to expert evidence.

4.3 Obtaining expert evidence will often be an expensive step and may take time, especially in specialised areas of medicine where there are limited numbers of suitable experts. Patients and health care providers, and their advisers, will therefore need to consider carefully how best to obtain any necessary expert help quickly and cost-effectively. Assistance with locating a suitable expert is available from a number of sources.

Use of experts (para 4.2): In *Oxley -v- Penwarden* (2000) (unreported) 21 July, CA the judge at first instance felt there was apparently a conflict between para 4.2 of the protocol and CPR r 35.7(1). The latter gives power to the court to direct that evidence on a particular issue be given by just one expert. The judge saw no reason to treat a clinical negligence claim differently from any other claim and imposed an order for a single expert to be used on the issue of causation. The case went to the Court of Appeal who allowed the appeal and restored an original order permitting each side to use its own expert. The court made clear there was no presumption in favour of a single joint expert. Mantell LJ felt this was eminently a case for each side to have its own expert evidence.

5 Alternative approaches to settling disputes

5.1 It would not be practicable for this protocol to address in any detail how a patient or their adviser, or health care provider, might decide which method to adopt to resolve the particular problem. However, the courts increasingly expect parties to try to settle their differences by agreement before issuing proceedings.

5.2 Most disputes are resolved by **discussion and negotiation**. Parties should bear in mind that carefully planned face-to-face meetings may be particularly helpful in exploring further treatment for the patient, in reaching understandings about what happened, and on both parties' positions, in narrowing the issues in dispute and, if the timing is right, in helping to settle the whole matter.

5.3 Summarised below are some other alternatives for resolving disputes:

- The revised **NHS Complaints Procedure,** which was implemented in April 1996, is designed to provide patients with an explanation of what happened and an apology if appropriate. It is not designed to provide compensation for cases of negligence. However, patients might choose to use the procedure if their only, or main, goal is to obtain an explanation, or to obtain more information to help them decide what other action might be appropriate.
- **Mediation** may be appropriate in some cases: this is a form of facilitated negotiation assisted by an independent neutral party. It is expected that the new Civil Procedure Rules will give the court the power to stay proceedings for 1 month for settlement discussions or mediation.
- Other methods of resolving disputes include **arbitration, determination by an expert, and early neutral evaluation** by a medical or legal expert. The Lord Chancellor's Department has produced a booklet on **'Resolving Disputes Without Going to Court',** LCD 1995, which lists a number of organisations that provide alternative dispute resolution services.

Annex A: Illustrative Flowchart

INITIAL STAGES

Patient (P)   Health care provider (HCP)

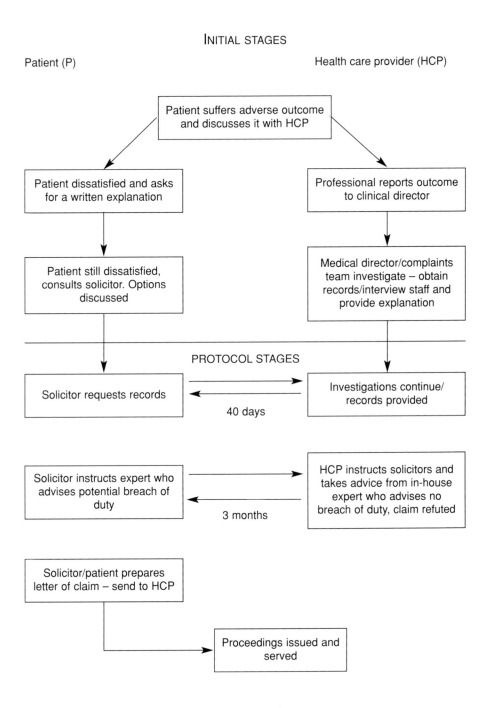

PROTOCOL STAGES

Annex B: Protocol for obtaining hospital medical records

Civil Litigation Committee © The Law Society June 1998

Application on behalf of a patient for hospital medical records for use when court proceedings are contemplated.

PURPOSE OF THE FORMS

The application form and response forms have been prepared by a working party of the Law Society's Civil Litigation Committee and approved by the Department of Health for use in NHS and Trust hospitals.

The purpose of the forms is to standardise and streamline the disclosure of medical records to a patient's solicitors, who are investigating pursuing a personal injury claim against a third party, or a medical negligence claim against the hospital to which the application is addressed and/or other hospitals or general practitioners.

USE OF THE FORMS

Use of the forms is entirely voluntary and does not prejudice any party's right under the Access to Health Records Act 1990, the Data Protection Act 1984, or ss 33 and 34 of the Supreme Court Act 1981. However, it is Department of Health policy that patients be permitted to see what has been written about them, and that health care providers should make arrangements to allow patients to see all their records, not only those covered by the Access to Health Records Act 1990. The aim of the forms is to save time and costs for all concerned for the benefit of the patient and the hospital and in the interests of justice. Use of the forms should make it unnecessary in most cases for there to be exchanges of letters or other enquiries. If there is any unusual matter not covered by the form, the patient's solicitor may write a separate letter at the outset.

CHARGES FOR RECORDS

The Access to Health Records Act 1990 prescribes a maximum fee of £10. Photocopying and postage costs can be charged in addition. No other charges may be made.

The NHS Executive guidance makes it clear to health care providers that 'it is a perfectly proper use' of the 1990 Act to request records in that framework for the purpose of potential or actual litigation, whether against a third party or against the hospital or Trust.

The 1990 Act does not permit differential rates of charges to be levied if the application is made by the patient, or by a solicitor on his or her behalf, or whether the response to the application is made by the health care provider directly (the medical records manager or a claims manager) or by a solicitor.

The NHS Executive guidance recommends that the same practice should be followed with regard to charges when the records are provided under a voluntary agreement as under the 1990 Act, except that in those circumstances the £10 access fee will not be appropriate.

The NHS Executive also advises:

- that the cost of photocopying may include 'the cost of staff time in making copies' and the costs of running the copier (but not costs of locating and sifting records)
- that the common practice of setting a standard rate for an application or charging an administration fee is not acceptable because there will be cases when this fails to comply with the 1990 Act.

RECORDS: WHAT MIGHT BE INCLUDED

X-rays and test results form part of the patient's records. Additional charges for copying X-rays are permissible. If there are large numbers of X-rays, the records officer should check with the patient/solicitor before arranging copying.

Reports on an 'adverse incident' and reports on the patient made for risk management and audit purposes may form part of the records and be discloseable: the exception will be any specific record or report made solely or mainly in connection with an actual or potential claim.

RECORDS: QUALITY STANDARDS

When copying records, health care providers should ensure:
- All documents are legible, and complete, if necessary by photocopying at less than 100% size.
- Documents larger than A4 in the original, e.g. ITU charts, should be reproduced in A3, or reduced to A4 where this retains readability.
- Documents are only copied on one side of paper, unless the original is two-sided.
- Documents should not be unnecessarily shuffled or bound and holes should not be made in the copied papers.

ENQUIRIES/FURTHER INFORMATION

Any enquiries about the forms should be made initially to the solicitors making the request.

Comments on the use and content of the forms should be made to the Secretary, Civil Litigation Committee, The Law Society, 113 Chancery Lane, London WC2A 1PL, telephone 020 730 5739, or to the NHS Management Executive, Quarry House, Quarry Hill, Leeds LS2 7UE, UK.

The Law Society,   May 1998

Application on behalf of a patient for hospital medical records for use when court proceedings are contemplated

This should be completed as fully as possible.

To: Medical Records Officer

Insert
Hospital   Hospital
Name
and
Address

1.
    (a) Full name of patient (including previous surnames)

    (b) Address now

    (c) Address at start of treatment

    (d) Date of birth (and death, if applicable)

    (e) Hospital ref no if available

    (f) N.I. number, if available

2.   This application is made because the patient is considering
    (a) a claim against your hospital as   YES/NO
          detailed in para 7 overleaf

          pursuing an action against   YES/NO
          someone else

3.   Department(s) where treatment was received

4.   Name(s) of consultant(s) at your hospital in charge of the treatment

5.   Whether treatment at your hospital was private or NHS, wholly or in part

6.   A description of the treatment received, with approximate dates

7.   If the answer to Q2(a) is
    'Yes' details of

(a) the likely nature of the claim

(b) grounds for the claim

(c) approximate dates of the events involved

8. If the answer to Q2(b) is
     'Yes' insert

    (a) the names of the proposed defendants

    (b) whether legal proceedings yet begun   YES/NO

    (c) if appropriate, details of the claim and action number

9. We confirm we will pay reasonable copying charges

10. We request prior details of
    (a) photocopying and
         administration charges
         for medical records   YES/NO

    (b) number of and cost of
         copying X-ray and scan films   YES/NO

11. Any other relevant
    information, particular
    requirements, or any
    particular documents not
    required (e.g. copies of
    computerised records)

    Signature of Solicitor
    Name
    Address
    Ref.
    Telephone number
    Fax number   *Please print name beneath each signature.*
                                   Signature by child over 12 but under 18 years
                                   also requires signature by parent

Signature of patient

Signature of parent or next friend if appropriate

Signature of personal representative where patient has died

First response to application for hospital records

NAME OF PATIENT

Our ref

Your ref

1. Date of receipt of
    patient's application

2. We intend that copy
    medical records will be   YES/NO
    dispatched within 6
    weeks of that date

3. We require pre-payment
    of photocopying charges   YES/NO

4. If estimate of
    photocopying charges
    requested or pre-payment
    required the amount will   £ / notified to you
    be

5. The cost of X-ray and   £ / notified to you
    scan films will be

6. If there is any problem,
    we shall write to you   YES/NO
    within those 6 weeks

7. Any other information

    Please address further
    correspondence to

    Signed
    Direct telephone number
    Direct fax number
    Dated

Second response enclosing patient's hospital medical records

Address

Our Ref
Your Ref

NAME OF PATIENT:

1. We confirm that the enclosed copy medical
    records are all those within the control of the
    hospital, relevant to the application which you   YES/NO
    have made to the best of our knowledge and
    belief, subject to paras 2–5 below

2. Details of any other documents which have
    not yet been located

3. Date by when it is expected that these will
    be supplied

4. Details of any records which we are not
    producing

5. The reasons for not doing so

6. An invoice for copying and
    administration charges is attached   YES/NO

    Signed

    Date

Annex C: Templates for letters of claim and response

CI: Letter of claim

ESSENTIAL CONTENTS

1. Client's name, address, date of birth, etc.
2. Dates of allegedly negligent treatment.
3. Events giving rise to the claim:
   - an outline of what happened, including details of other relevant treatments to the client by other health care providers.
4. Allegation of negligence and causal link with injuries:
   - an outline of the allegations or a more detailed list in a complex case
   - an outline of the causal link between allegations and the injuries complained of.
5. The client's injuries, condition and future prognosis.
6. Request for clinical records (if not previously provided):
   - use the Law Society form if appropriate or adapt
   - specify the records required
   - if other records are held by other providers, and may be relevant, say so
   - state what investigations have been carried out to date, e.g. information from client and witnesses, any complaint and the outcome, if any clinical records have been seen or expert's advice obtained.
7. The likely value of the claim
   - an outline of the main heads of damage, or, in straightforward cases, the details of loss.

OPTIONAL INFORMATION

- What investigations have been carried out.
- An offer to settle without supporting evidence.
- Suggestions for obtaining expert evidence.
- Suggestions for meetings, negotiations, discussion or mediation.

POSSIBLE ENCLOSURES

- Chronology
- Clinical records request form and client's authorisation
- Expert report(s)
- Schedules of loss and supporting evidence.

C2: Letter of response

ESSENTIAL CONTENTS

1. Provide requested records and invoice for copying:
   - explain if records are incomplete or extensive records are held and ask for further instructions
   - request additional records from third parties.
2. Comments on events and/or chronology:
   - if events are disputed or the health care provider has further information or documents on which they wish to rely, these should be provided, e.g. internal protocol
   - details of any further information needed from the patient or a third party should be provided.
3. If breach of duty and causation are accepted:
   - suggestions might be made for resolving the claim and/or requests for further information
   - a response should be made to any offer to settle.
4. If breach of duty and/or causation are denied:
   - a bare denial will not be sufficient. If the health care provider has other explanations for what happened, these should be given at least in outline
   - suggestions might be made for the next steps, e.g. further investigations, obtaining expert evidence, meetings/negotiations or mediation, or an invitation to issue proceedings.

OPTIONAL MATTERS

- An offer to settle if the patient has not made one, or a counter offer to the patient's with supporting evidence.

POSSIBLE ENCLOSURES

- Clinical records
- Annotated chronology
- Expert reports.

Annex D: Lord Woolf's recommendations

1. Lord Woolf in his Access to Justice Report in July 1996, following a detailed review of the problems of medical negligence claims, identified that one of the major sources of costs and delay is at the pre-litigation stage because:
   - Inadequate incident reporting and record keeping in hospitals, and mobility of staff, make it difficult to establish facts, often several years after the event.
   - Claimants must incur the cost of an expert in order to establish whether they have a viable claim.
   - There is often a long delay before a claim is made.
   - Defendants do not have sufficient resources to carry out a full investigation of every incident, and do not consider it worthwhile to start an investigation as soon as they receive a request for records, because many cases do not proceed beyond that stage.
   - Patients often give the defendant little or no notice of a firm intention to pursue a claim. Consequently, many incidents are not investigated by the defendants until after proceedings have started.
   - Doctors and other clinical staff are traditionally reluctant to admit negligence or apologise to, or negotiate with, claimants for fear of damage to their professional reputations or career prospects.

2. Lord Woolf acknowledged that under the present arrangements health care providers, faced with possible medical negligence claims, have a number of practical problems to contend with:
   - Difficulties of finding patients' records and tracing former staff, which can be exacerbated by late notification and by the health care provider's own failure to identify adverse incidents.
   - The health care provider may have only treated the patient for a limited time or for a specific complaint: the patient's previous history may be relevant but the records may be in the possession of one of several other health care providers.
   - The large number of potential claims do not proceed beyond the stage of a request for medical records, or an explanation; and that it is difficult for health care providers to investigate fully every case whenever a patient asks to see the records.

Annex E: How to contact the Forum

The Clinical Disputes Forum

Chairman:
Dr Alastair Scotland
Medical Director and Chief Officer
National Clinical Assessment Authority
9th Floor, Market Towers
London
SW8 5NQ
Telephone: 020 7273 0850

Secretary:
Sarah Leigh
c/o Margaret Dangoor
3 Clydesdale Gardens
Richmond
Surrey
TW1O 5EG
Telephone: 020 8408 1012

Appendix 4

Useful addresses and websites

Action for Victims of Medical Accidents
44 High Street,
Croydon CRO 1YB
Tel: 020 8686 8333
http://www.avma.org.uk

British Medical Association
BMA House
Tavistock Square
London WC1H 9JP
Tel: 020 7387 4499
http://www.bma.org.uk

Commission for Health Improvement
10th Floor, Finsbury Tower
103–105 Bunhill Row
London EC1Y 8TG
Tel: 020 7448 9200
http://www.chi.nhs.uk

Council for Professions Supplementary to Medicine
Park House
184 Kennington Road
London SE11 4BU
Tel: 020 7582 0866
http://www.cpsm.org.uk

General Dental Council
37 Wimpole Street
London W1G 8DQ
Tel: 020 7887 3800
http://www.gdc-uk.org

General Medical Council
178 Great Portland Street
London W1W 5JE
Tel: 020 7580 7642
http://www.gmc-uk.org

Medical Defence Union
230 Blackfriars Road
London SE1 8PJ
Tel: 0800 716646
http://www.the-mdu.com/

Medical Protection Society
33 Cavendish Square
London W1G 0PS
Tel: 020 7399 1300
http://www.mps.org.uk

National Institute for Clinical Excellence
11 Strand
London WC2N 5HR
Tel: 020 7766 9191
http://www.nice.org.uk

Office of the Health Service Ombudsman
Millbank Tower
Millbank
London SW1P 4QP
Tel: 020 7217 4051/4068
http://www.ombudsman.org.uk/hse/england/make-complaint.html

Office of the Health Service Ombudsman for Wales
5th Floor, Capital Tower
Greyfriars Road
Cardiff CF10 3AG
Tel: 0845 601 0987/029 2022 6909
http://www.ombudsman.org.uk/hse/wales/make-complaint.html

Royal Pharmaceutical Society of Great Britain
1 Lambeth High Street
London SE1 7JN
Tel: 020 7735 9141
http://www.rpsgb.org.uk

United Kingdom Central Council for Nursing, Midwifery and Health Visiting
23 Portland Place
London W1B 1PZ
Tel: 020 7637 7181
http://www.ukcc.org.uk

Index

Page numbers in **bold** refer to case summaries.